www.nescafe.co.uk

tick tock tick tock tick tock tick tock tick tock tick tock tick tock tick tock tick tock tick tock ticktock tick tock tick tock tick tock tick tock tick tock tick tock tick tock tick tock tick tock ticktock tick tock tick tock tick tock tick tock tick tock

tick tock tick tock tick tock tick ticktock tick tock tick tock tick tock tick tock tick tock tick tock tick tock tick tock tick tock tick tock slurp **24 hours** ck tick tock tick tock tick tock tick tock tick tock tick tock tick ti

tick tock tick tock tick tock tick tock tick tock tick tock tick tock tick tock tick tock tick tock ticktock tick tock tick tock tick tock tick tock tick tock tick tock tick tock tick tock ticktock tick tock tick tock tick tock tick tock tick tock tick tock ticktock tick tock tick tock tick tock tick

tick tock tick tock tick tock tick tock tick tock tick tock ticktock tick tock tick tock tick tock tick tock tick tock tick tock tick tock tick tock tick tock tick tock ticktock tick tock tick tock tick tock tick tock tick tock tick tock tick tock ticl

From start to end, any day is no more than an amalgamation of glimpsed moments - here 'daily life', in all its staged and spontaneous variation, has been captured by a host of young British photographers. The differing interpretations of the brief, set by Nescafé, testify to the creativity of the next crop of photographers hoping to join the profession.

'24 hours' was promoted as a competition through the pages of Dazed & Confused magazine, the independent publication that spawned such award-winning photographers as Rankin, Phil Poynter and Nick Waplington. Its commitment to discovering new talent and belief in the ethos of independence has been successfully built over time, whilst working with commercial partners to forward these aims.

The ability of these amateur and student photographers to work with a commercial brief - documenting the day-to-day omnipresence of a cup of the black stuff - demonstrates that one needn't fall back on the obvious when faced with the challenge of satisfying both the client and the artist's need for self-expression. The results are a study of the unspoken balance struck between selling a product and developing a creative working approach, allowing these artists to explore their ideas with honesty and enthusiasm.

That this book turns this theme into a playful, meditative, and always skilled collection bodes well for the futures of these talented new photographers. And the facilitation of this process by Nescafé and Dazed & Confused is as good an introduction to the working world as anyone can hope for. The best images were awarded prizes of up to £1,000, whilst the exposure and experience is more valuable for all those who can feel proud to have their work included in this book.

Dazed & Confused is pleased to invite you to look at the following pages. As our sponsors might suggest, put the kettle on and relax for a few minutes. We hope you like what you see.

0000

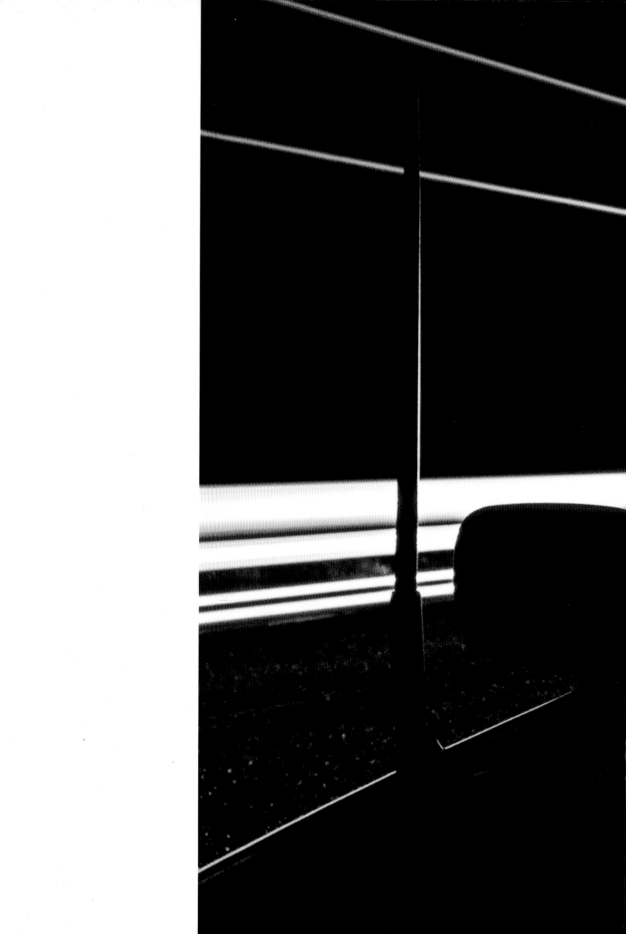

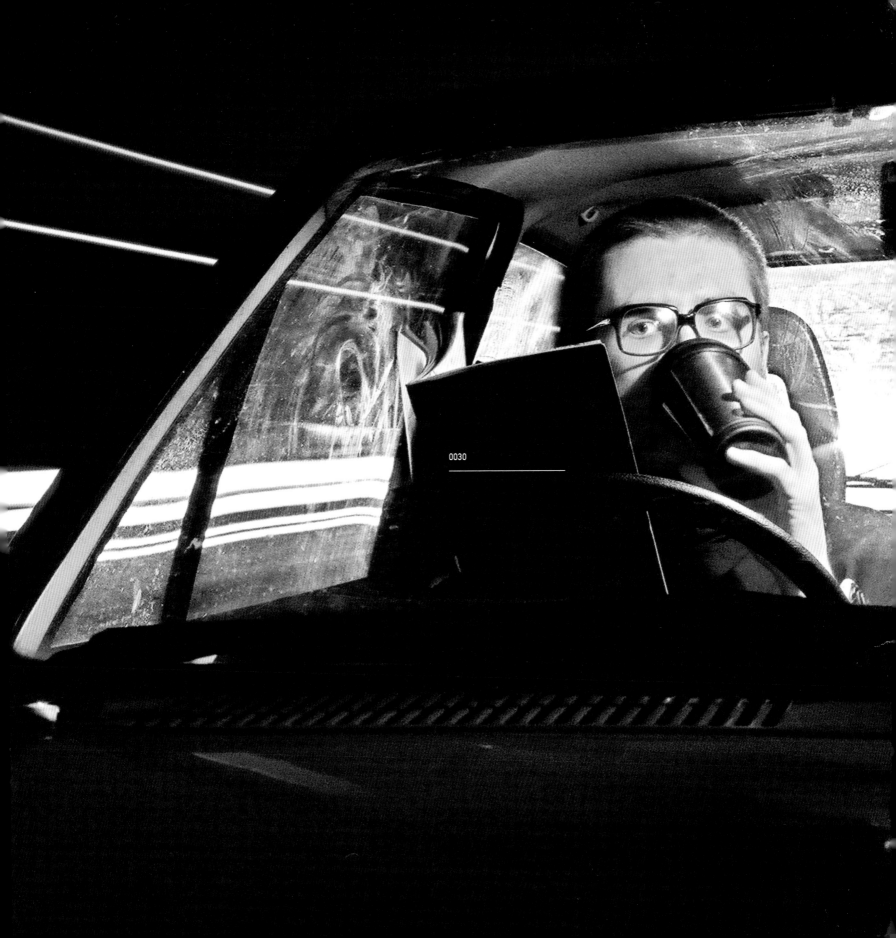

0030

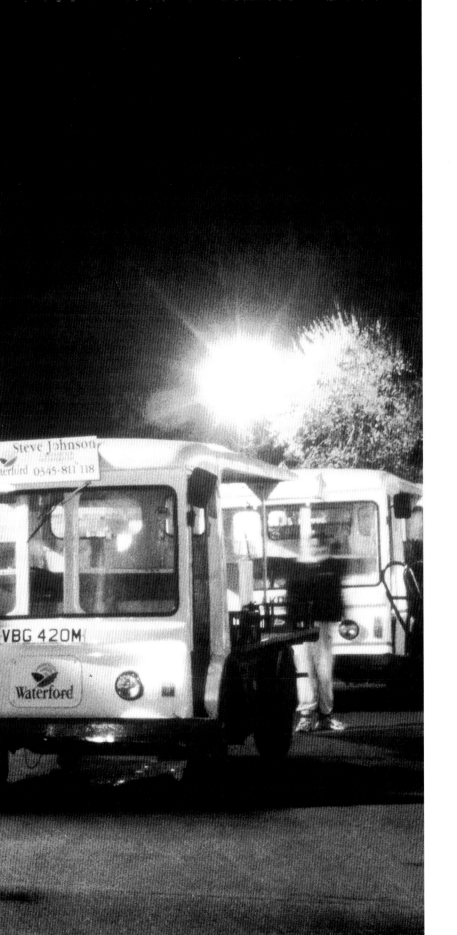

0215

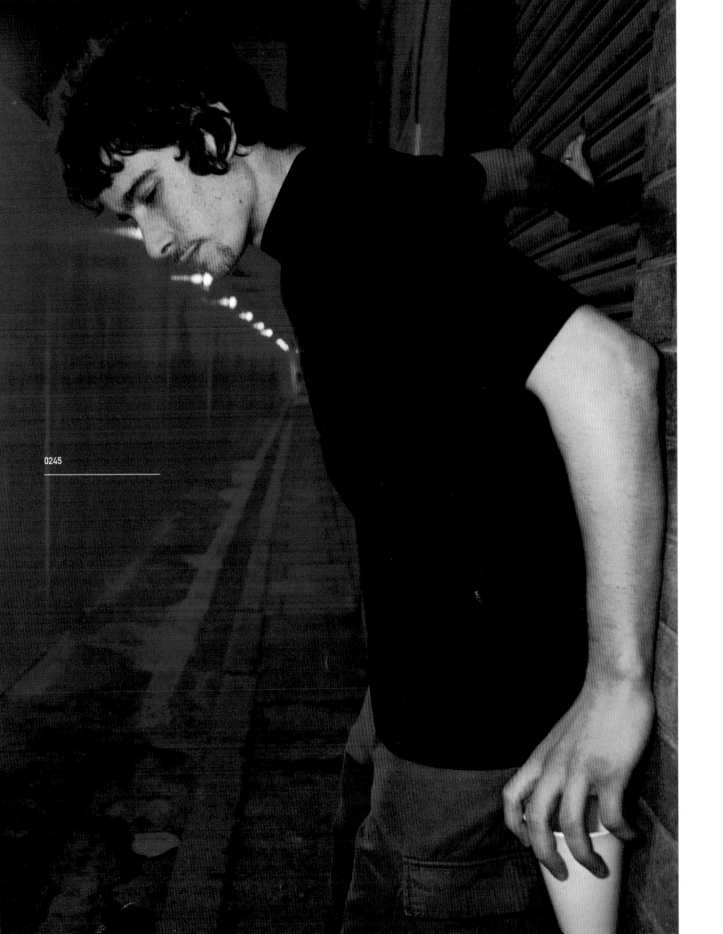

0245

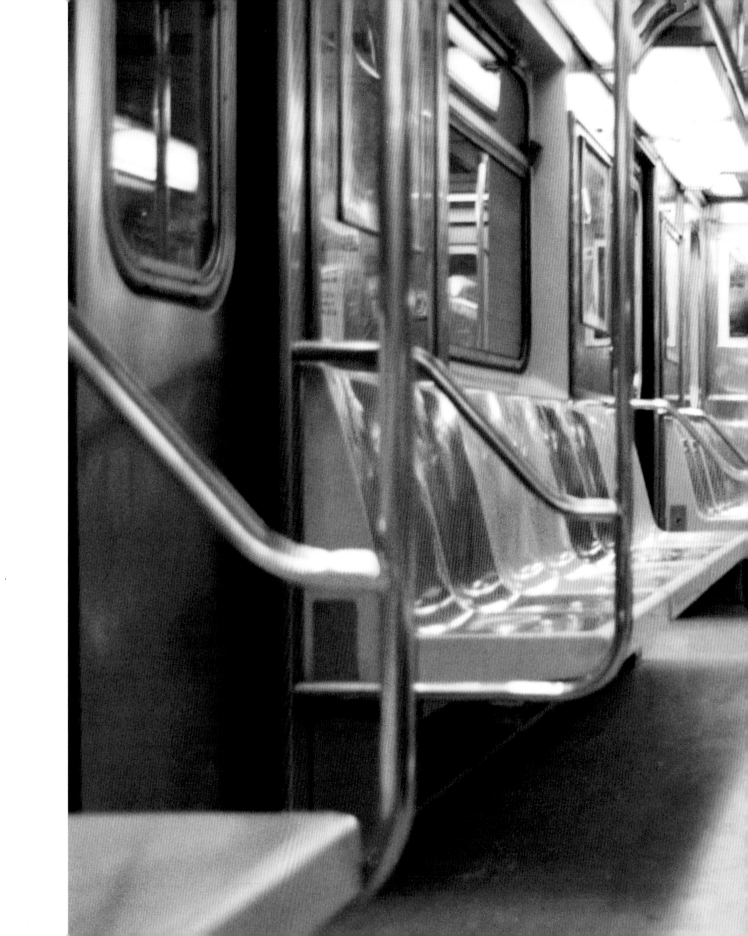

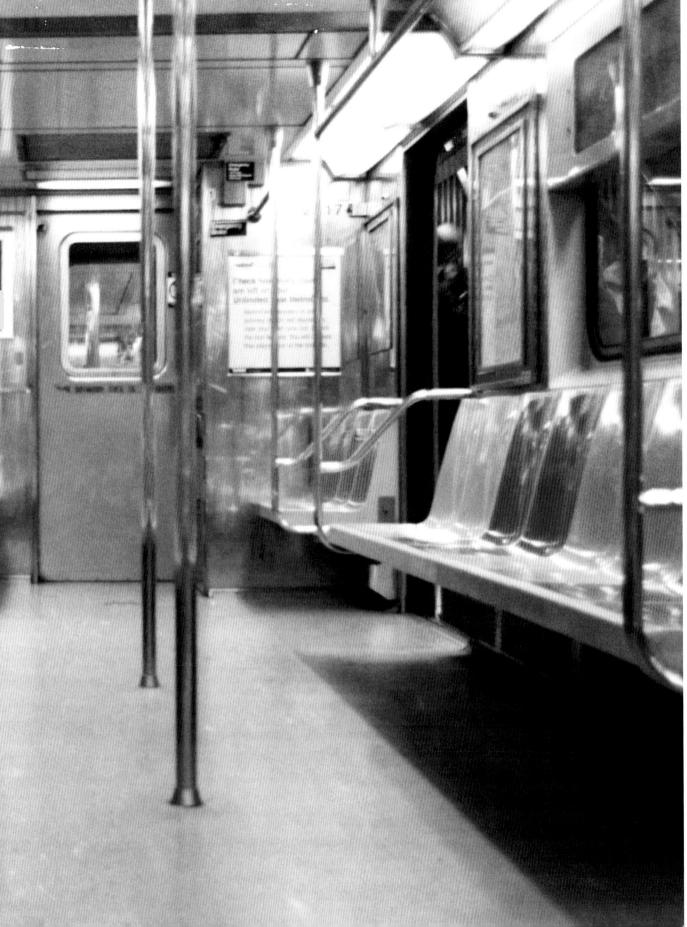

0246

0414

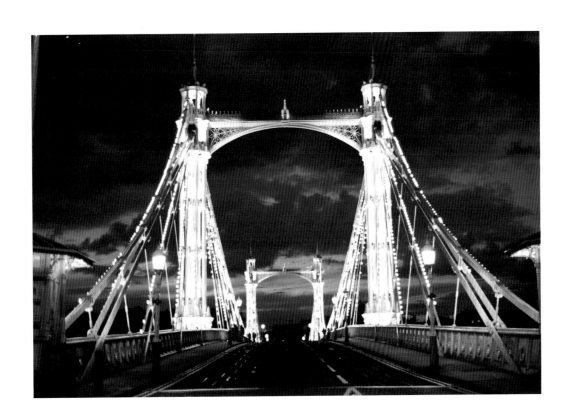

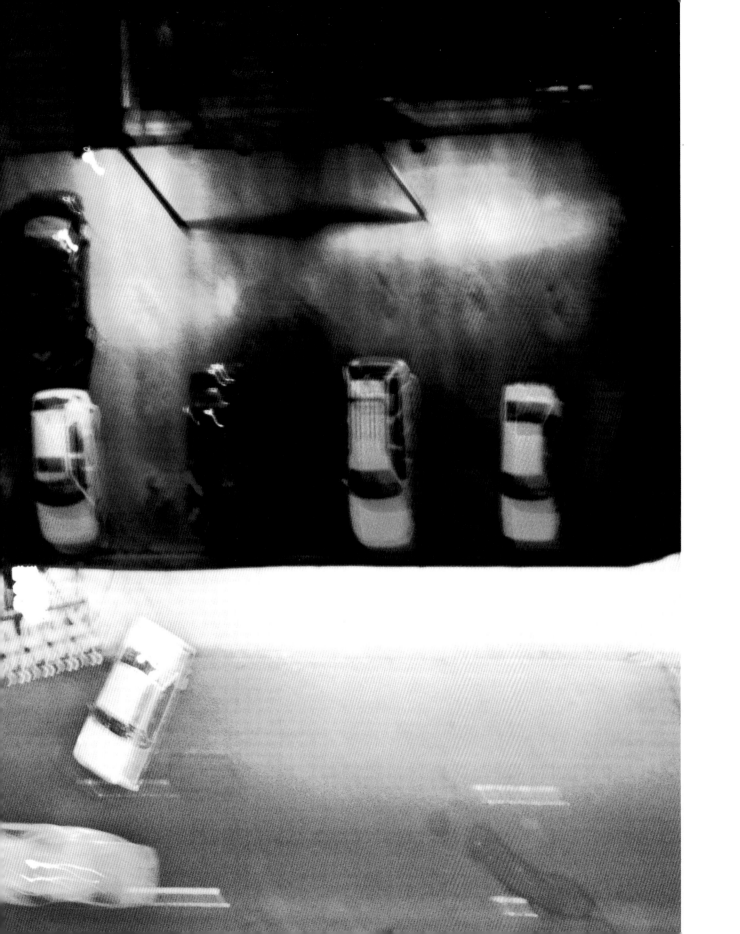

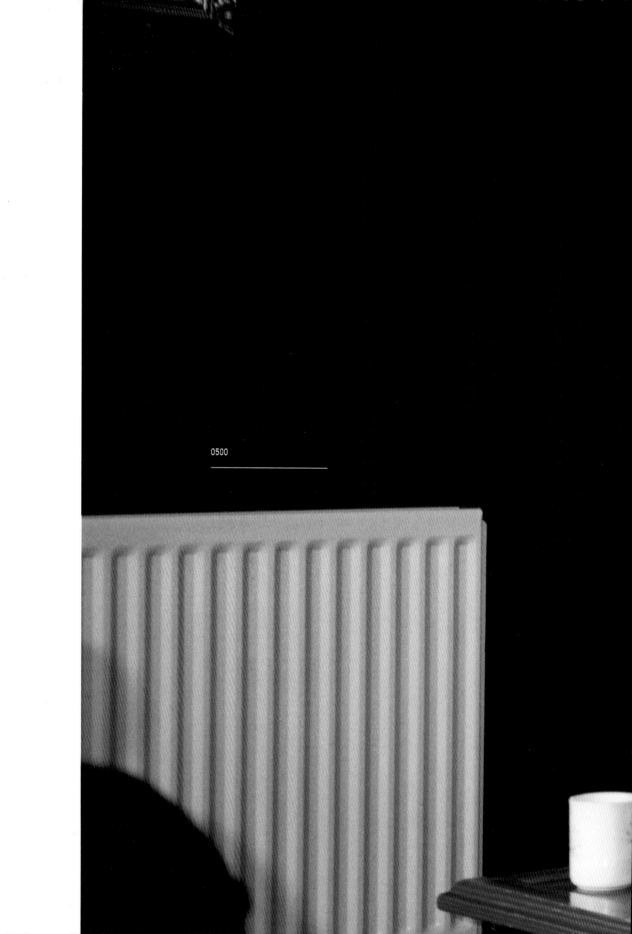

0500

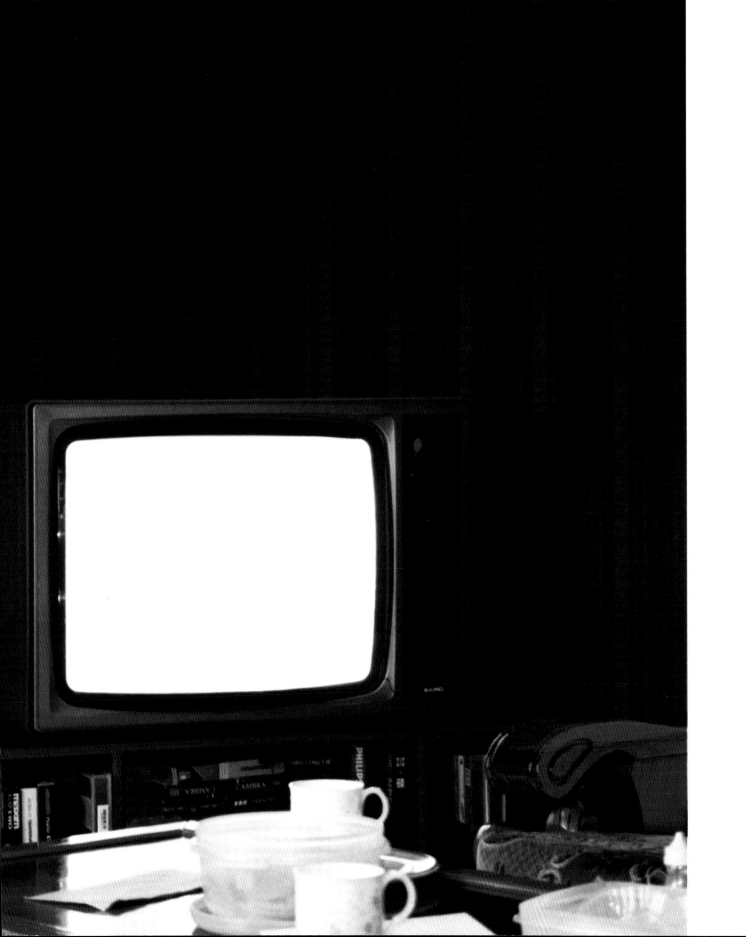

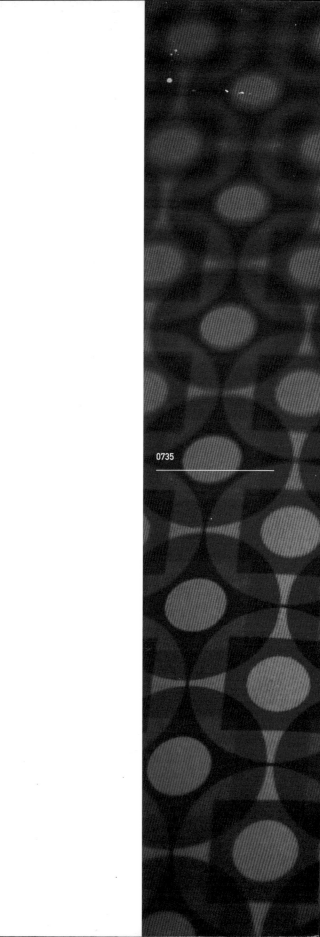

0735

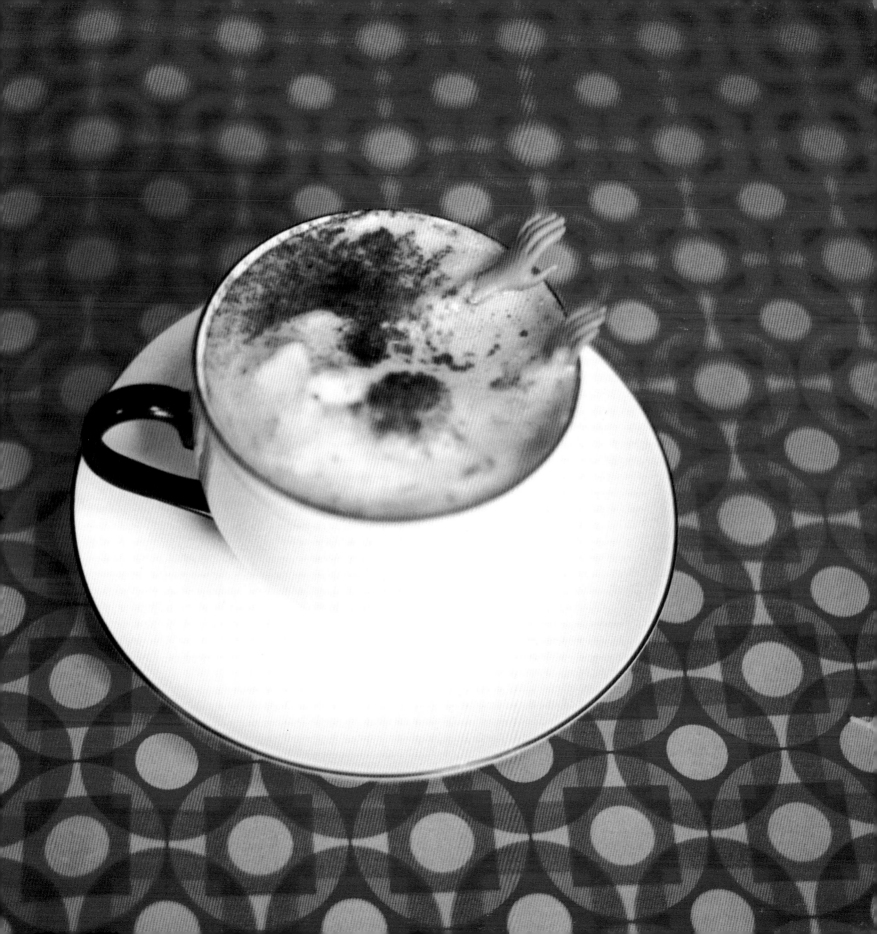

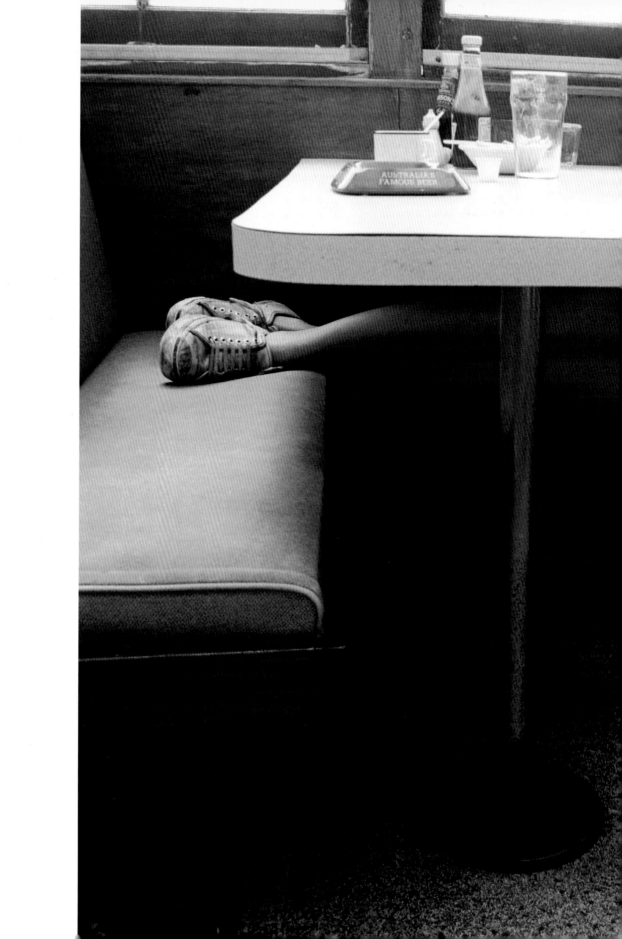

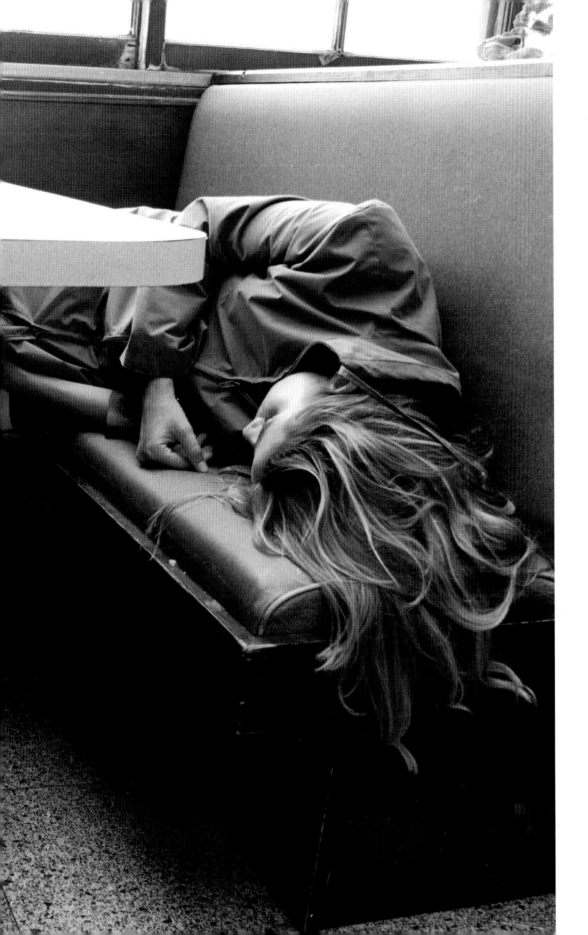

0800

0944

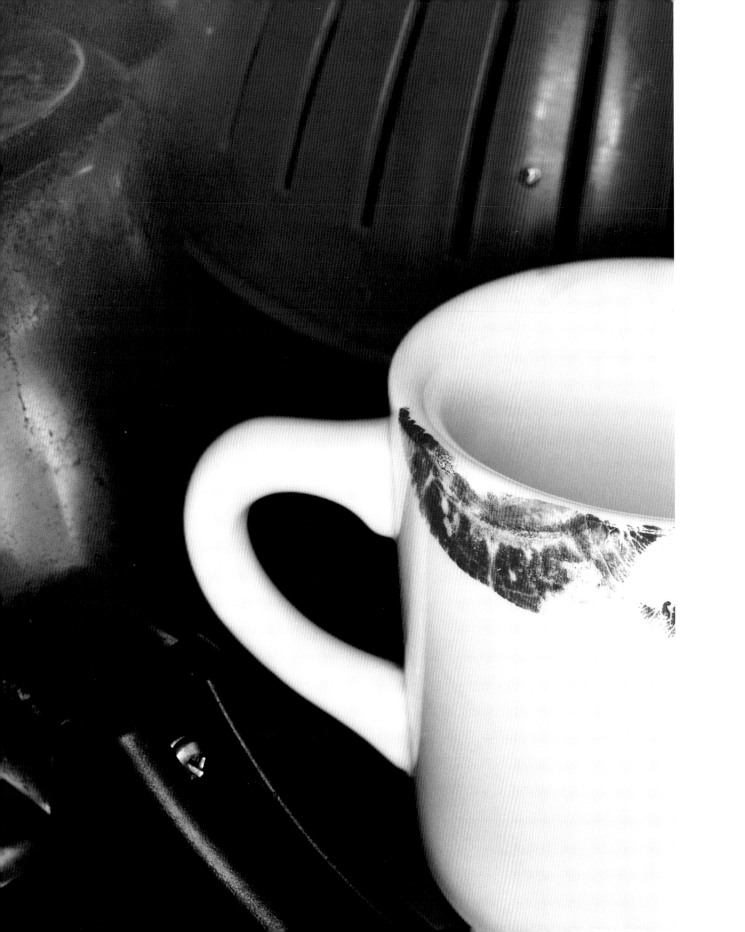

0954

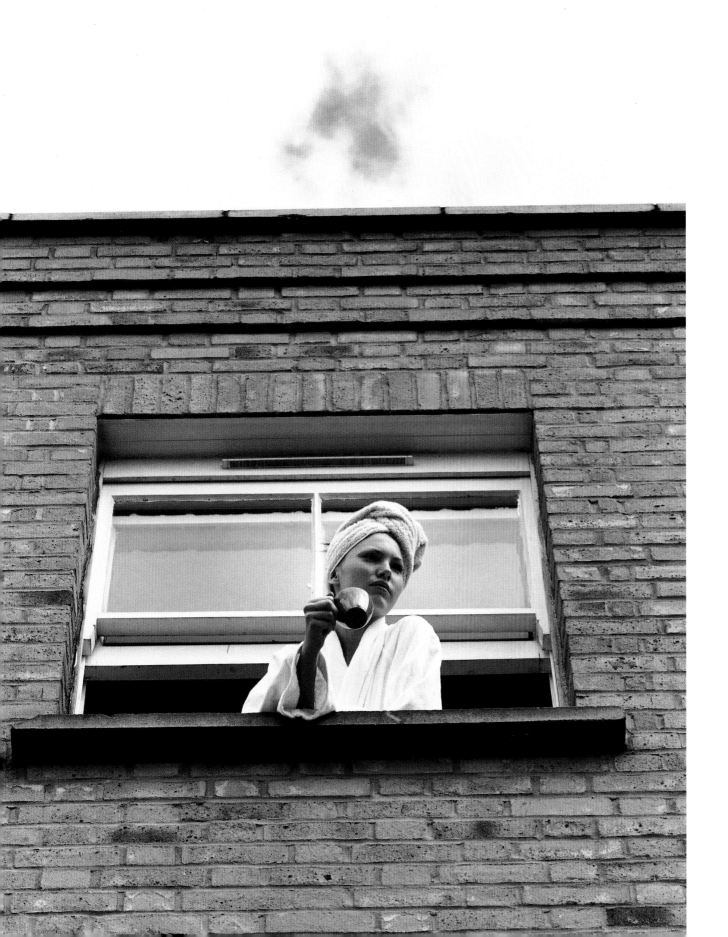

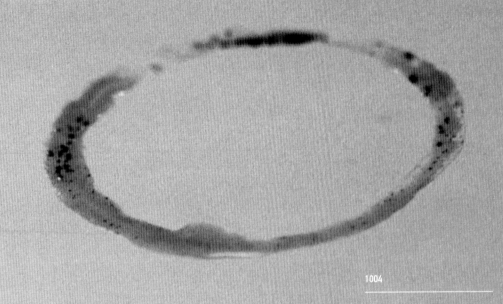

1004

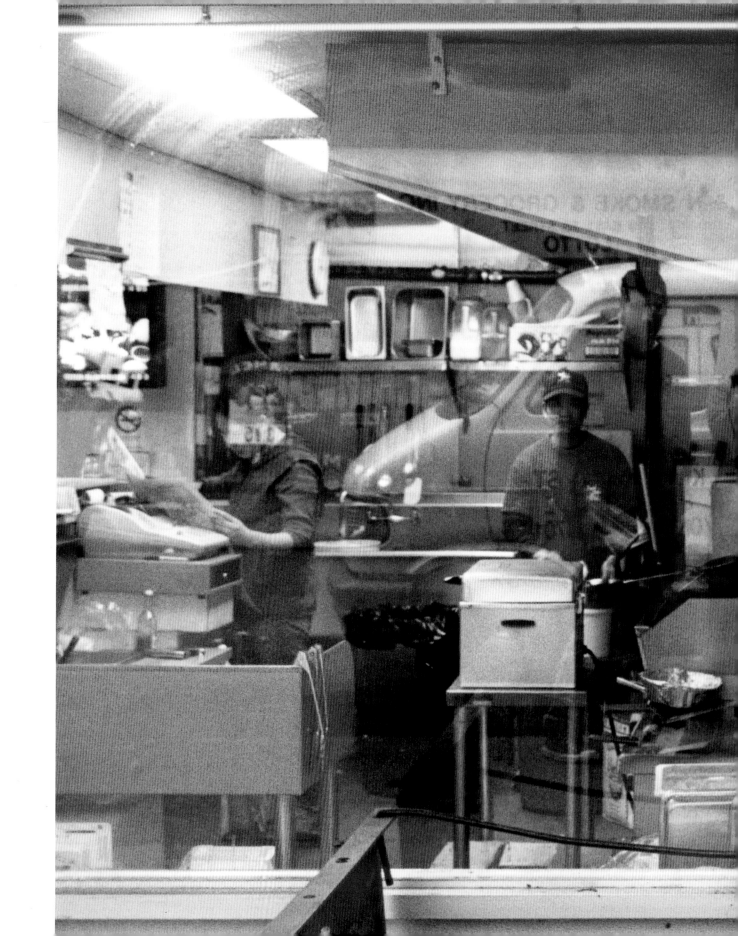

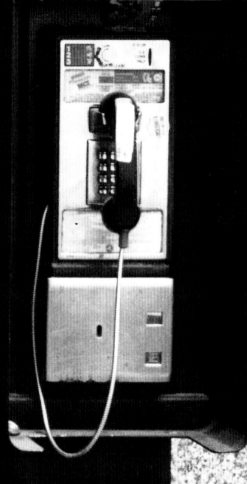

1006

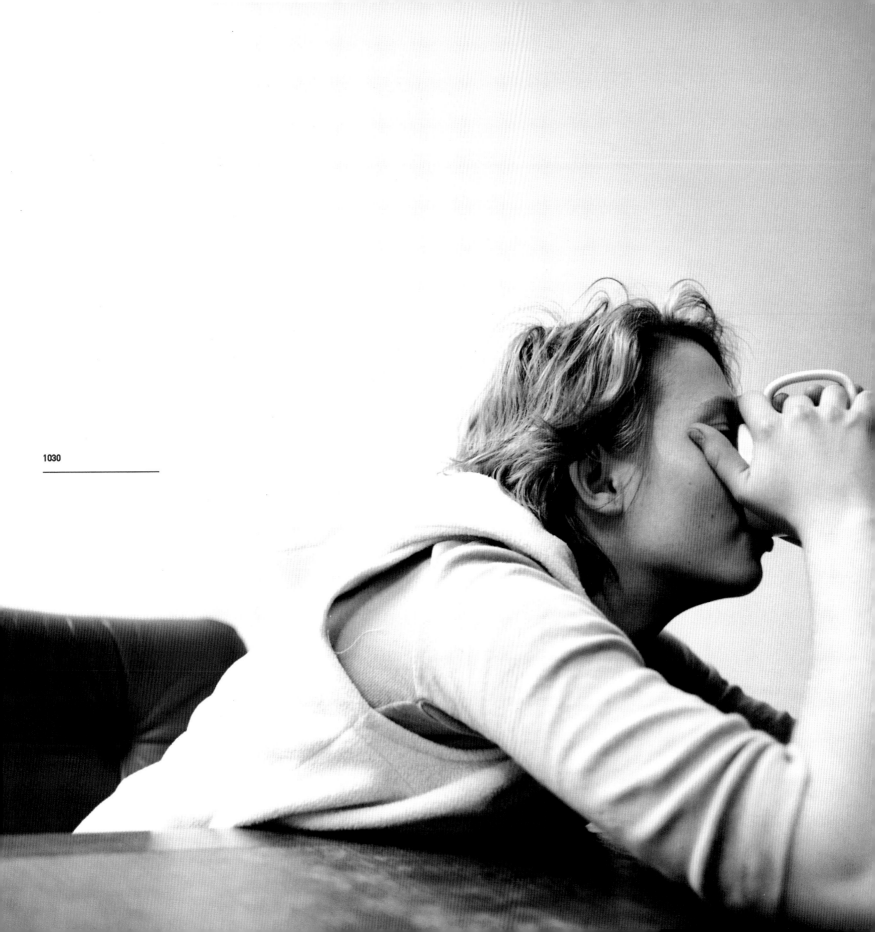

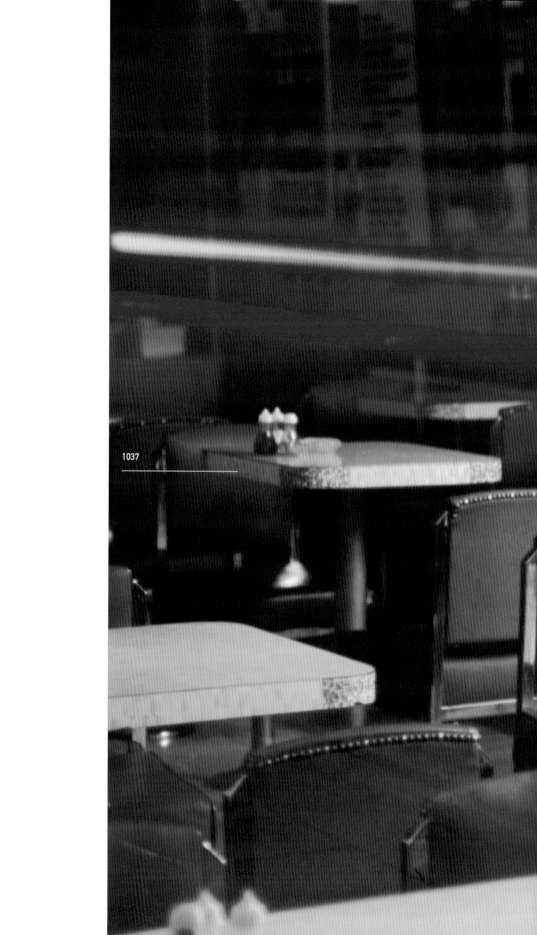

1037

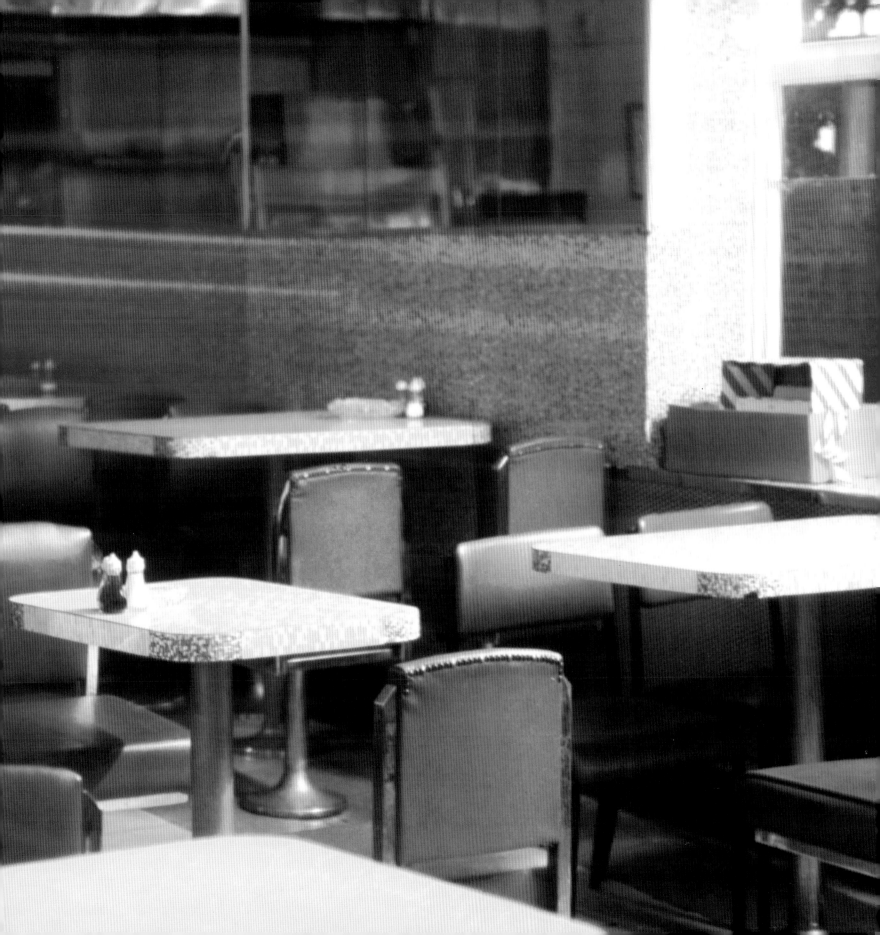

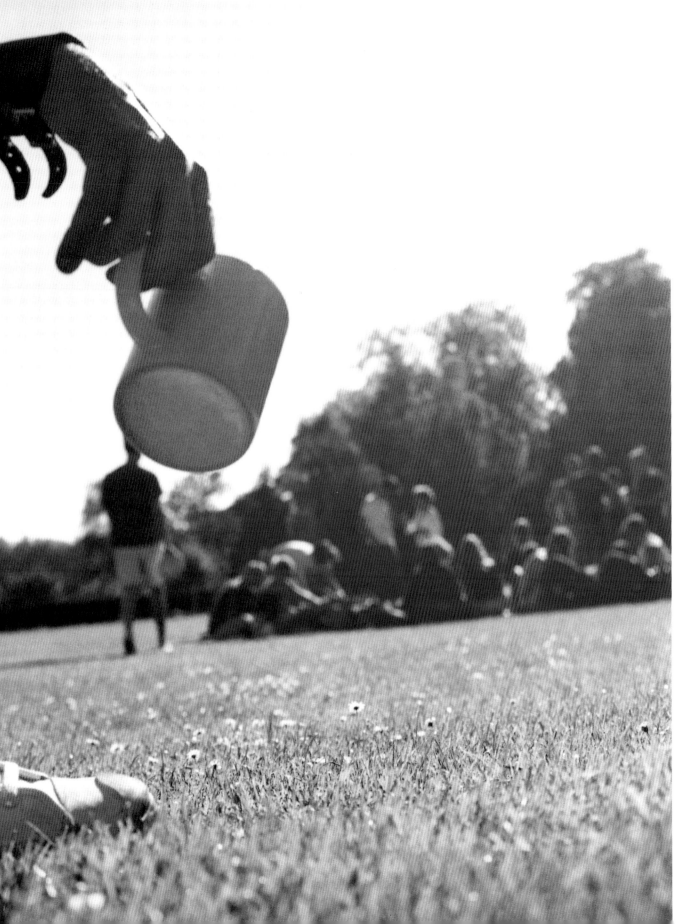

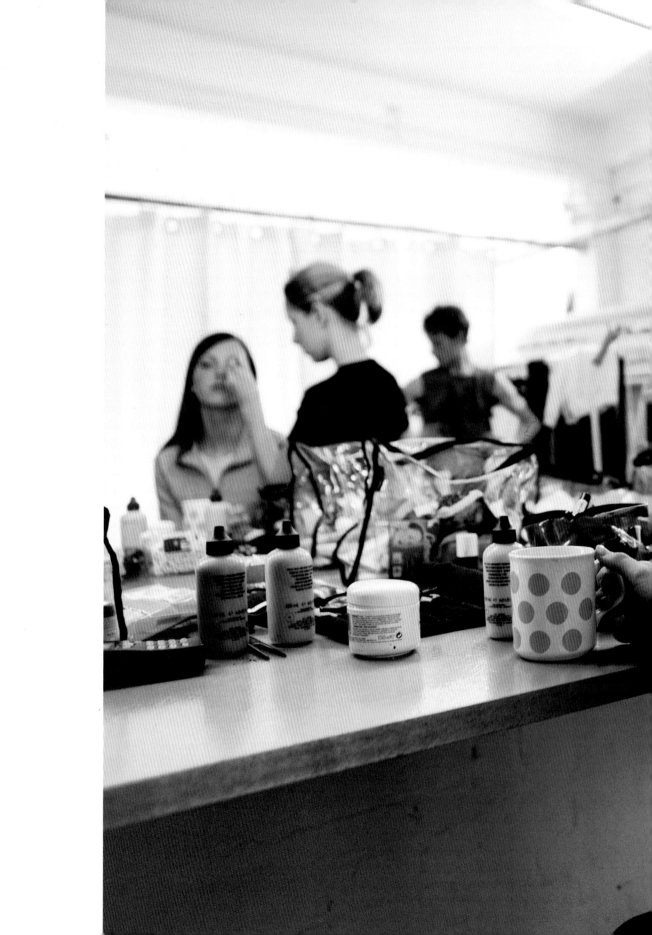

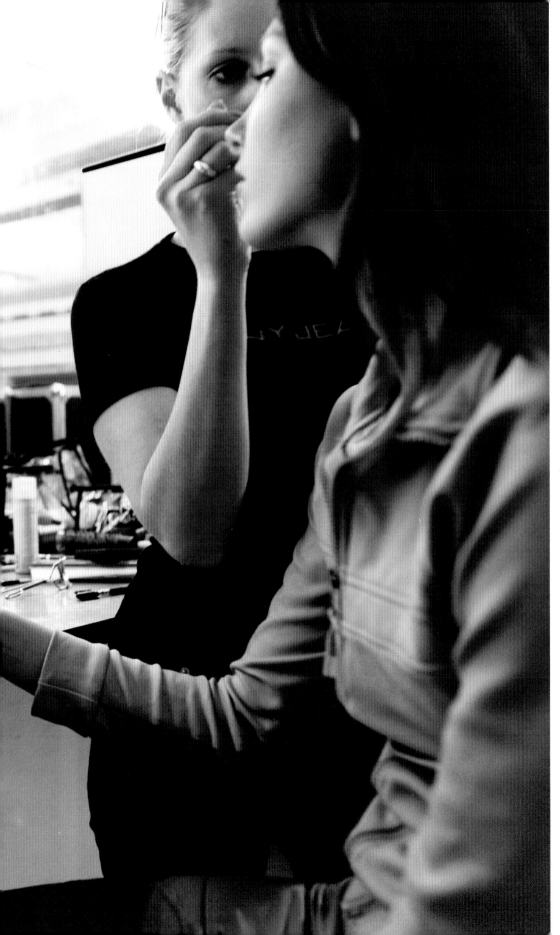

1155

1203

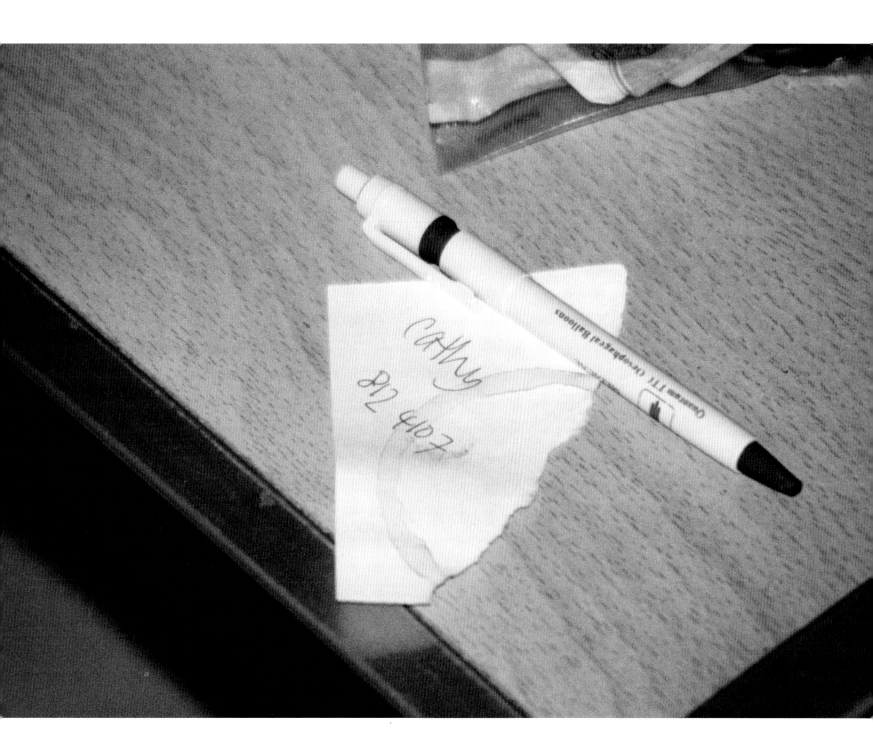

1315

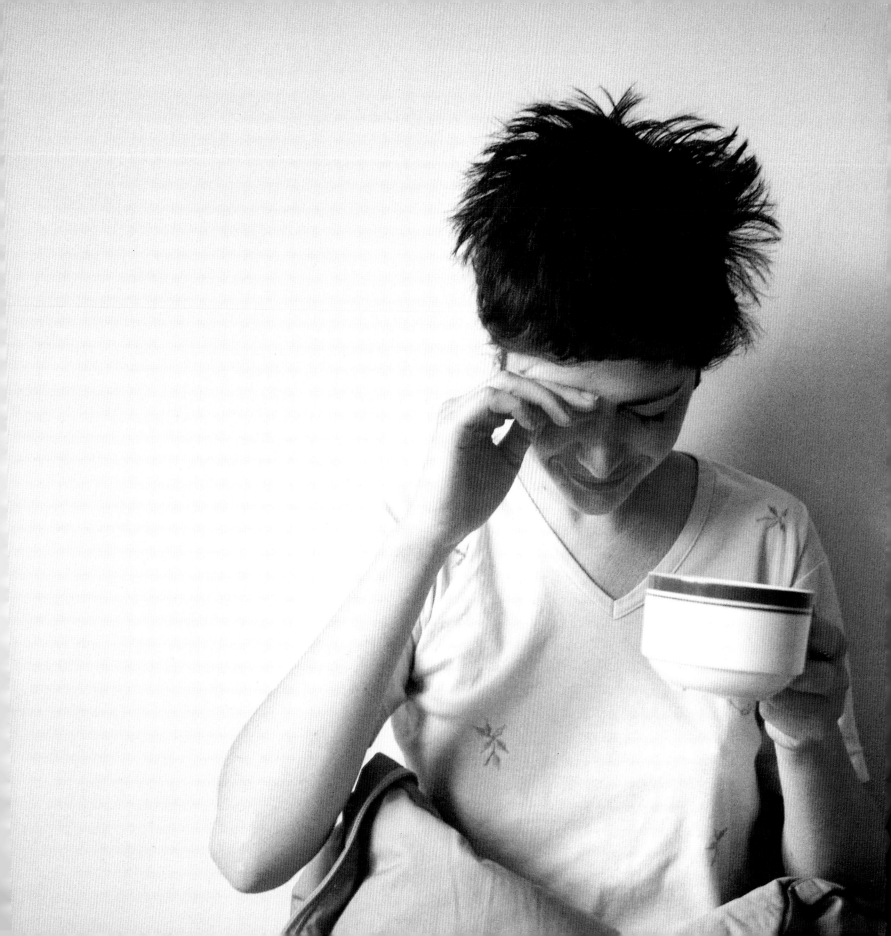

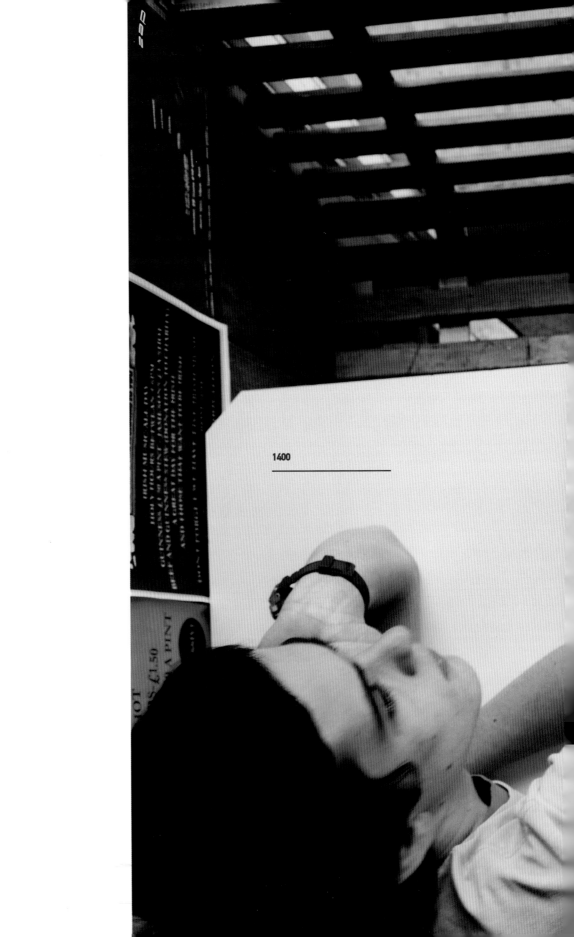

1400

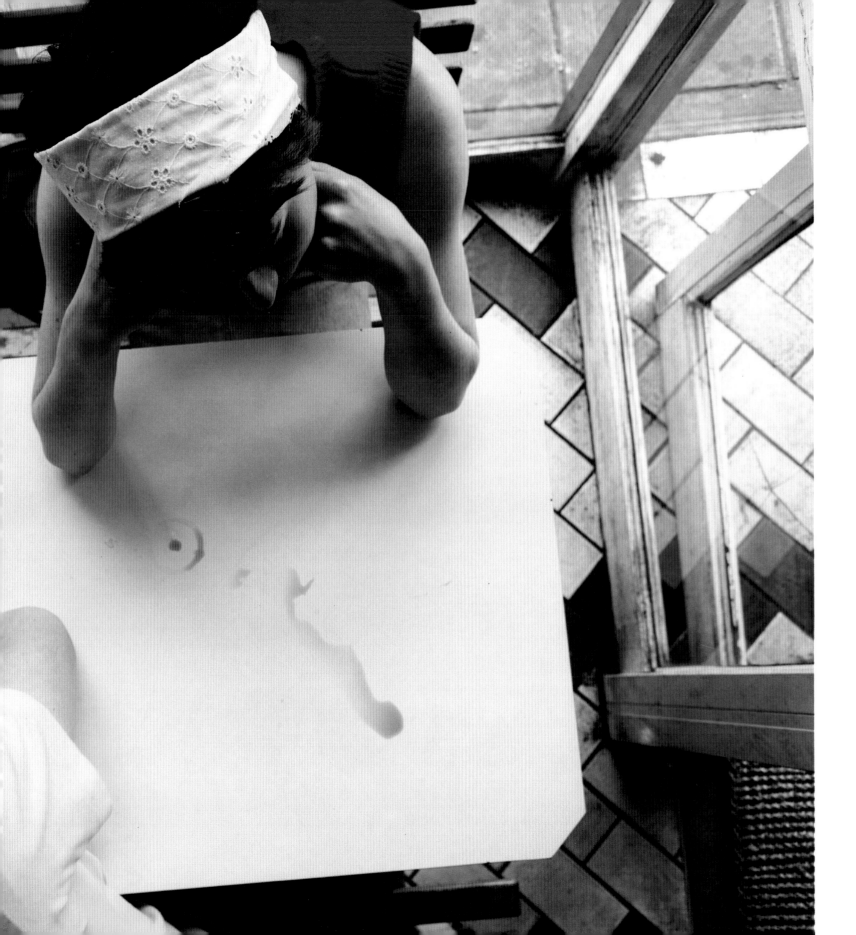

1412

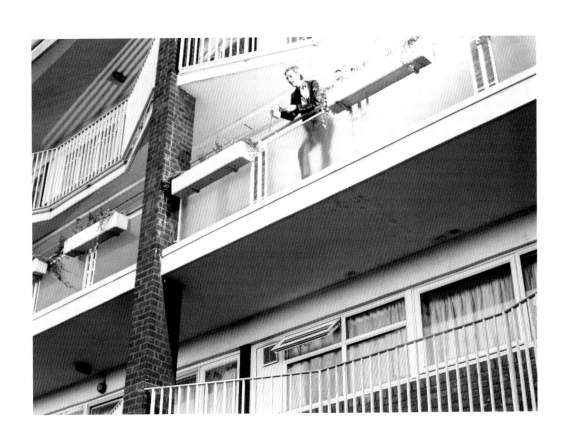

1430

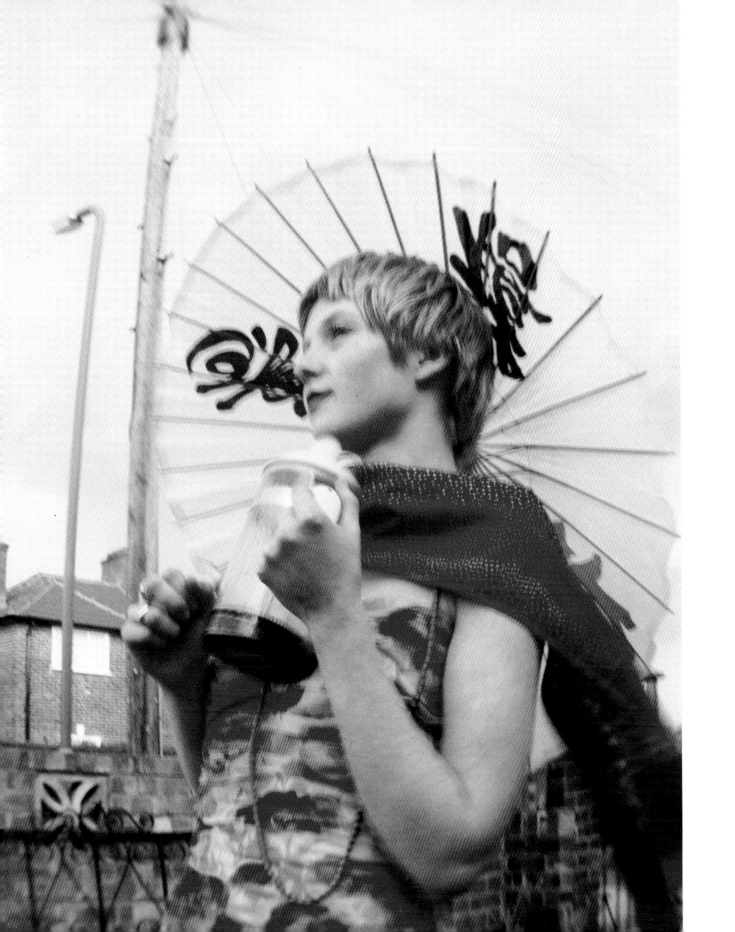

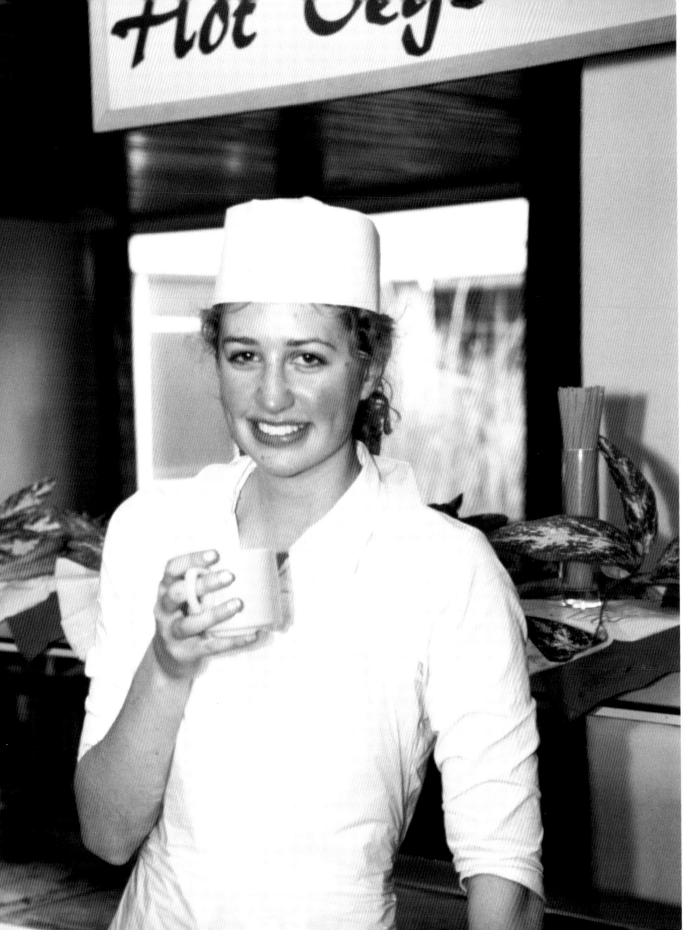

1439

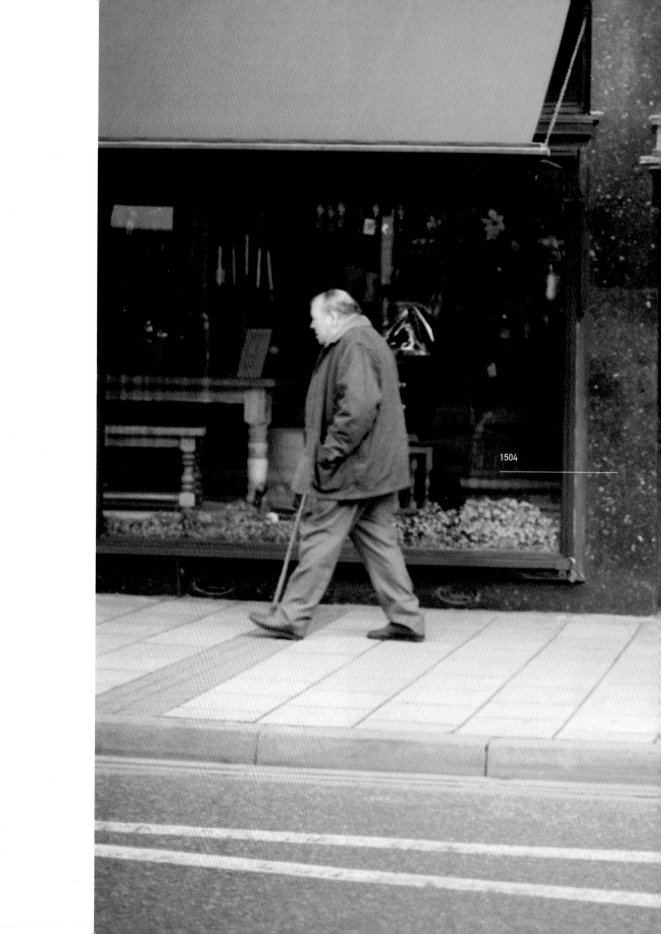

1504

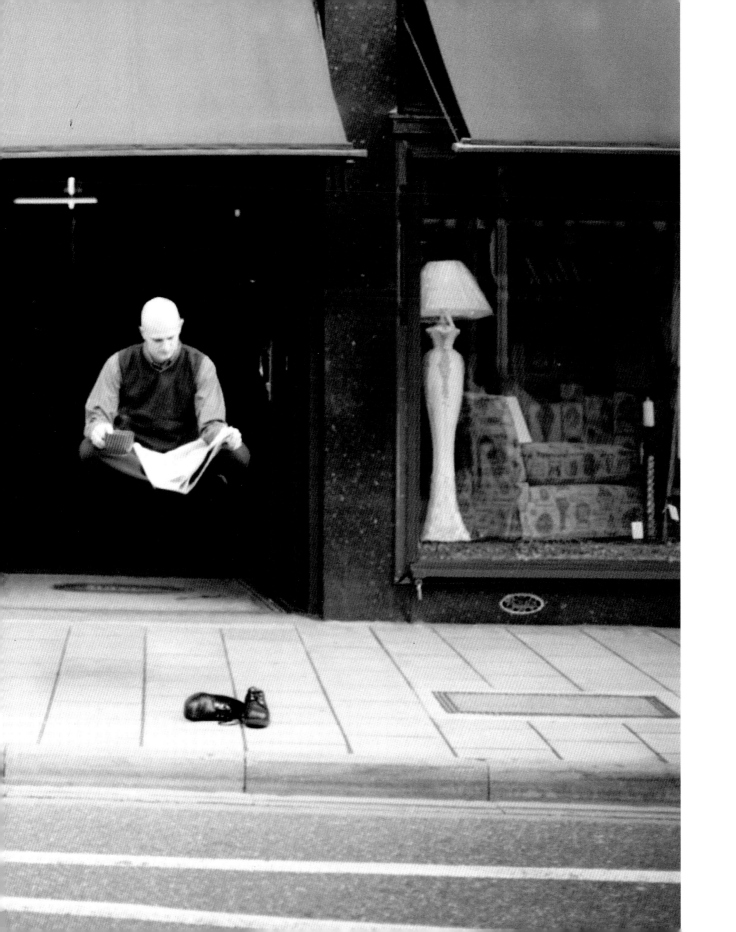

1509

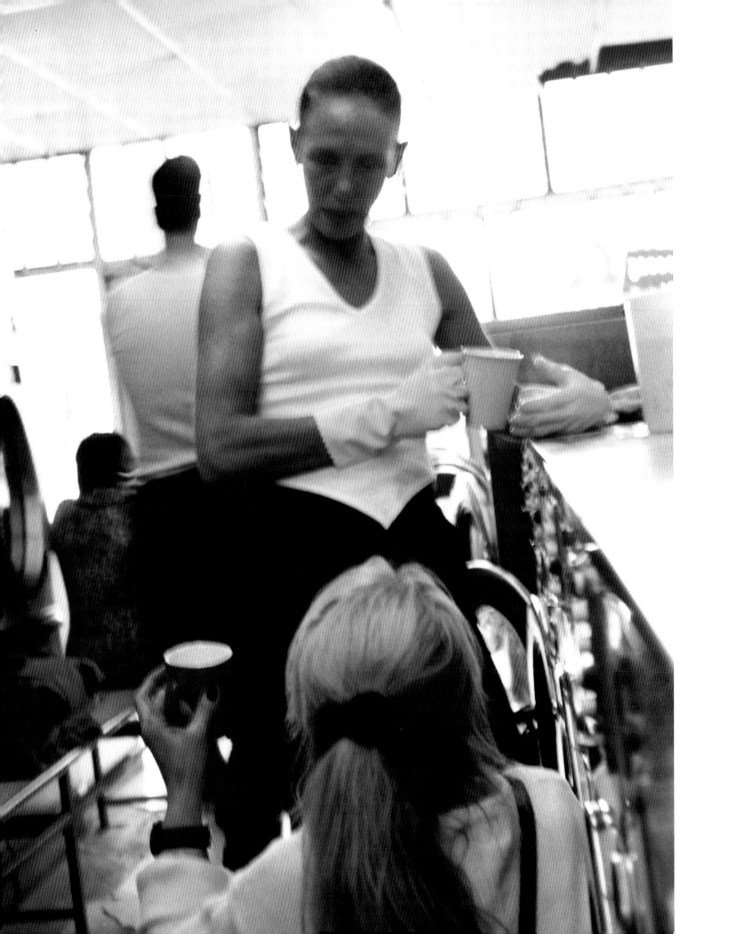

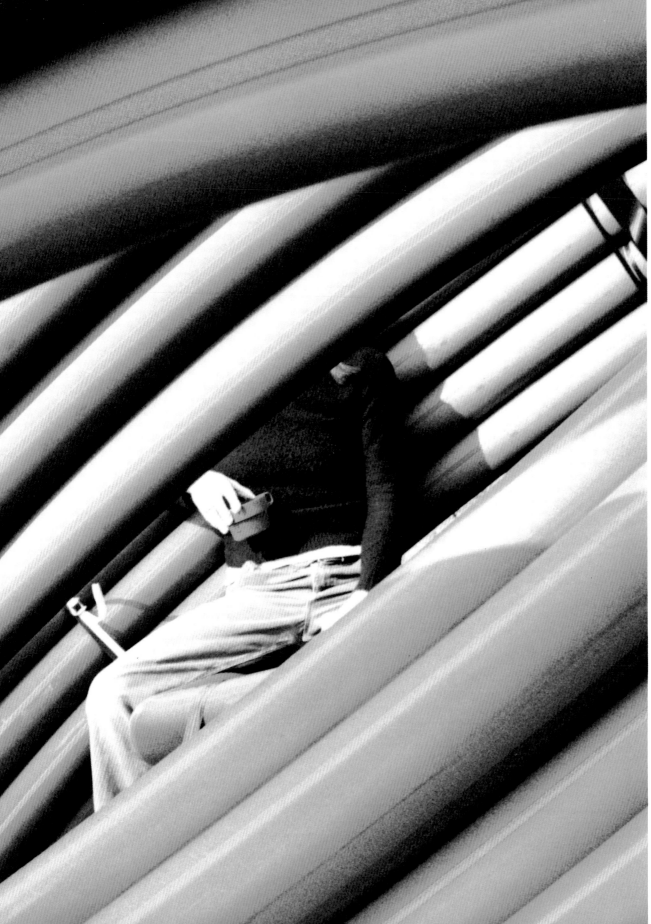

1537 45/46

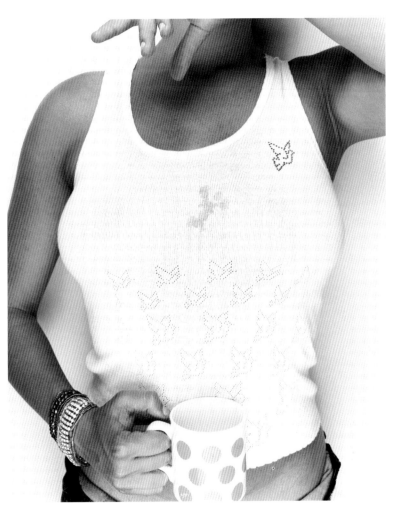 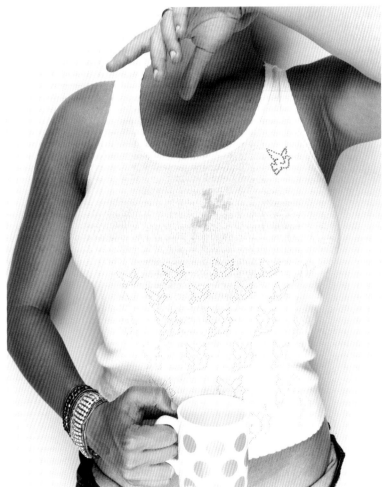

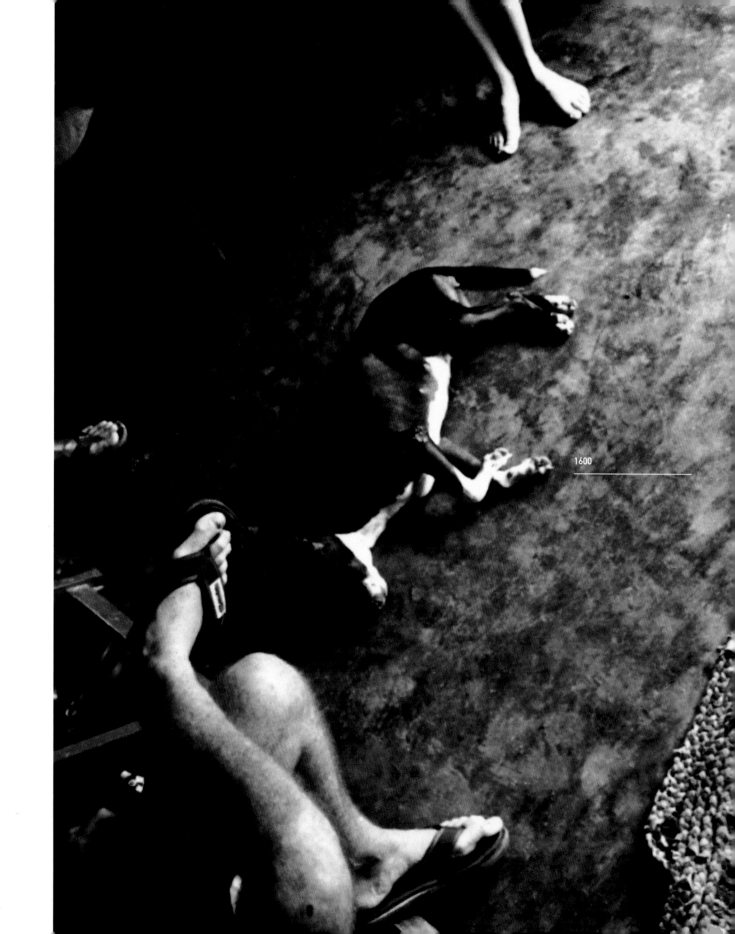

1600

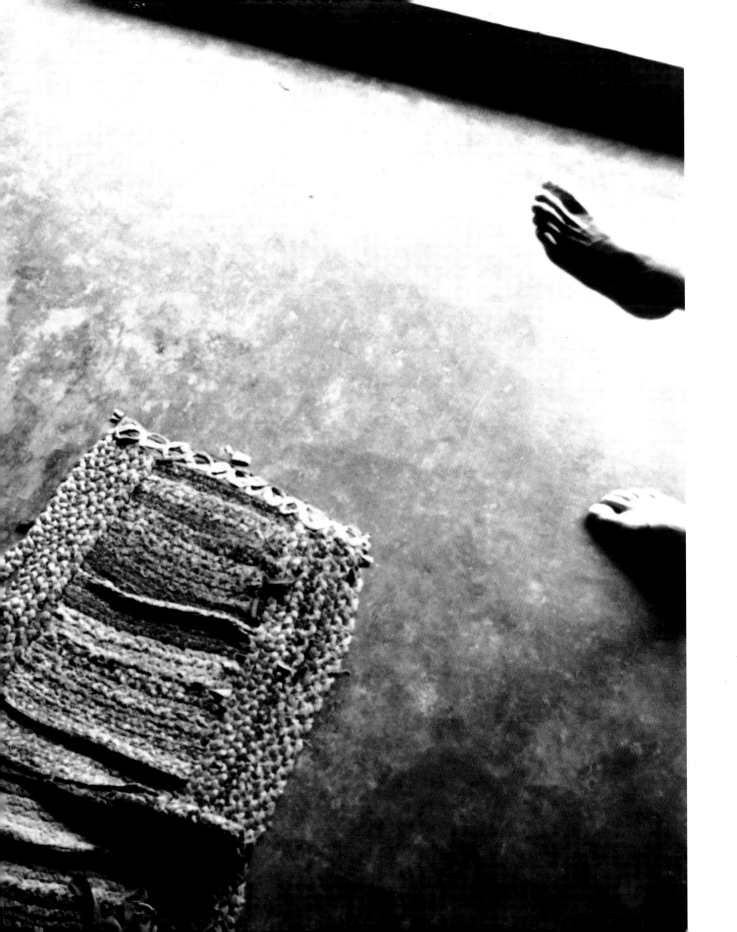

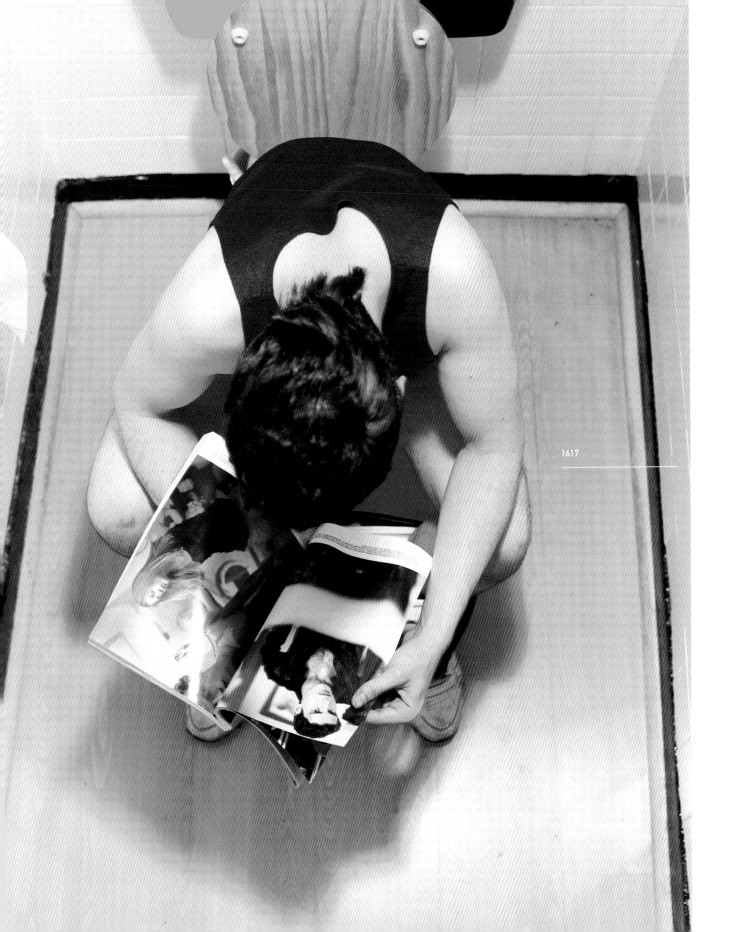

1617

1618

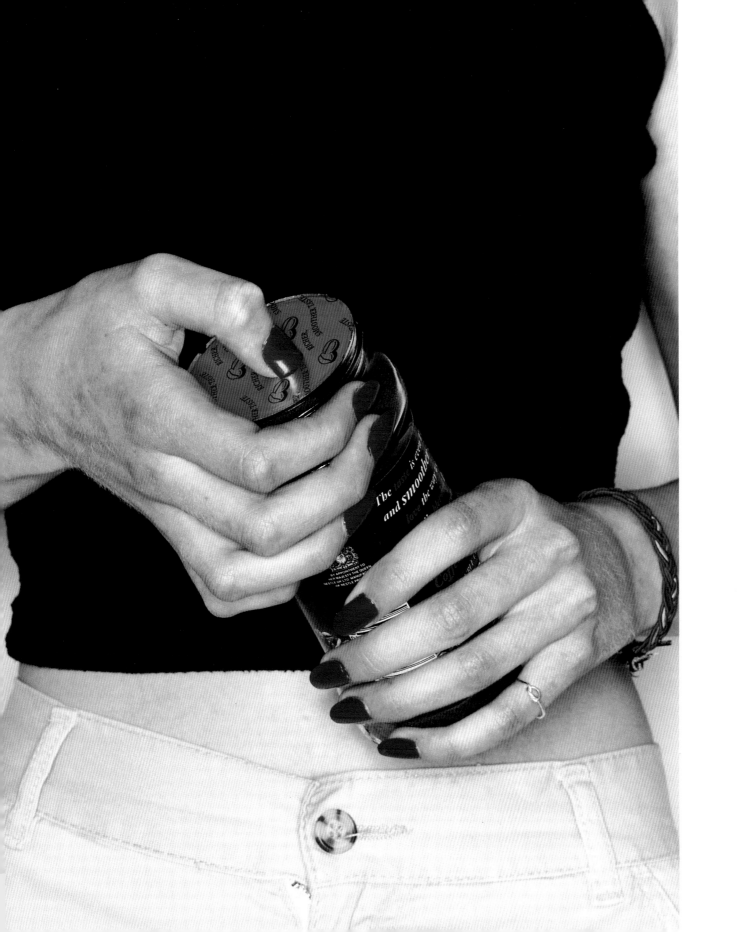

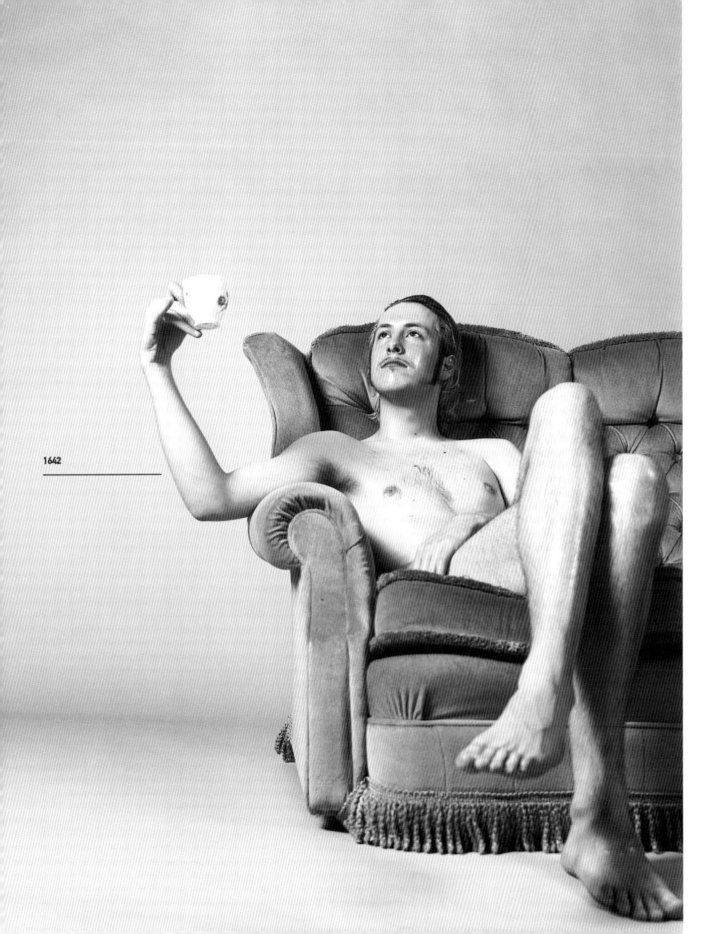

1642

1740

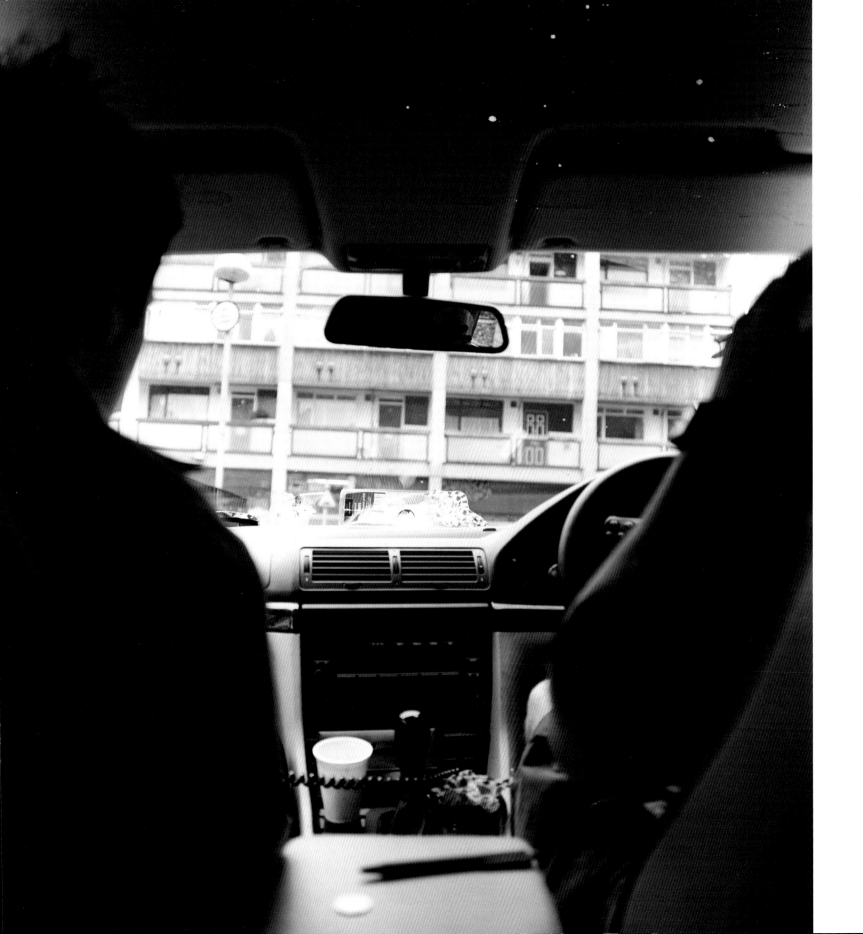

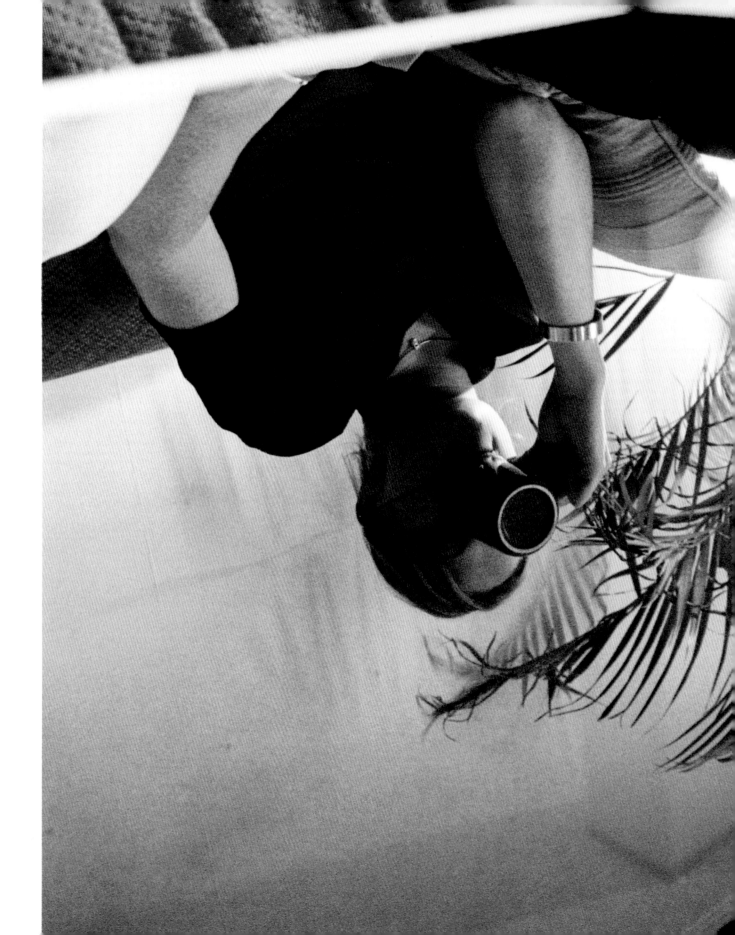

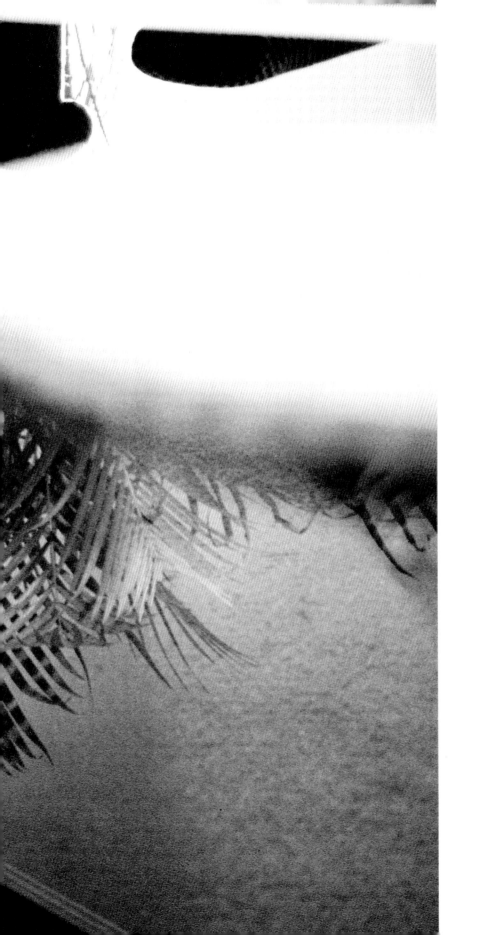

1831

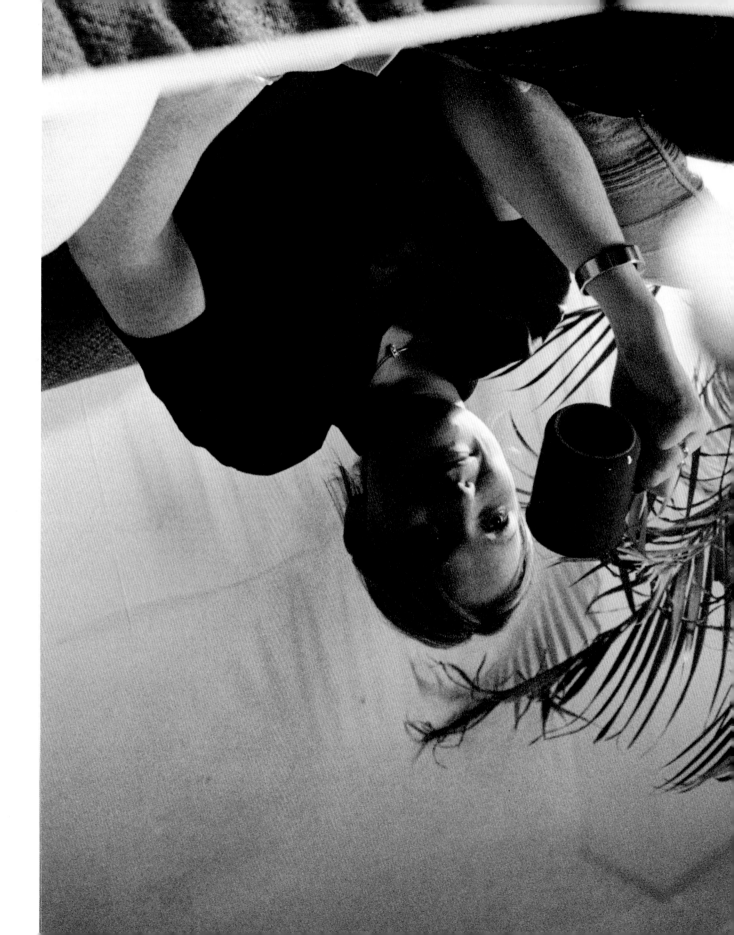

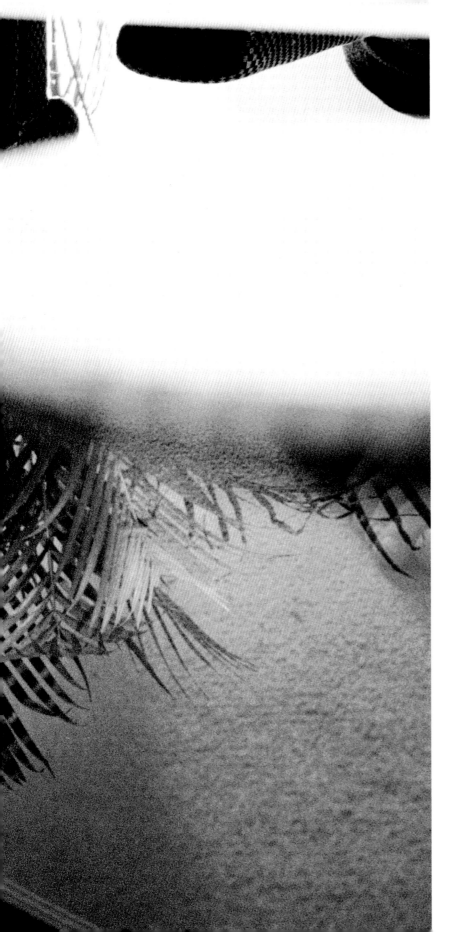

1834

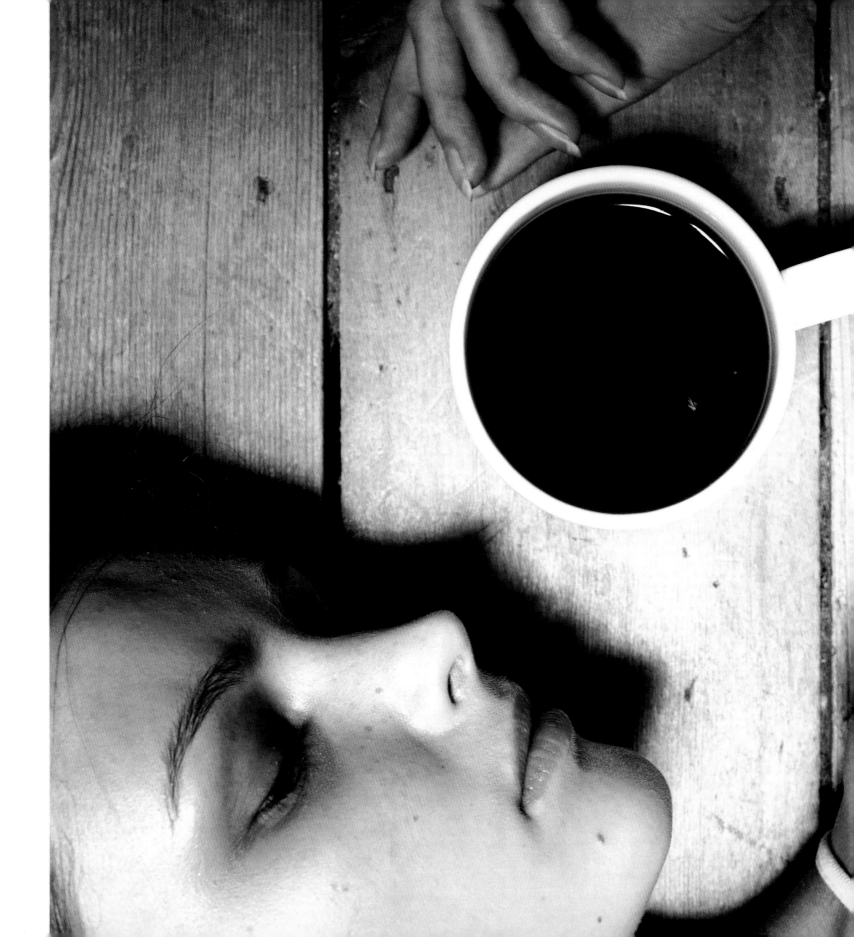

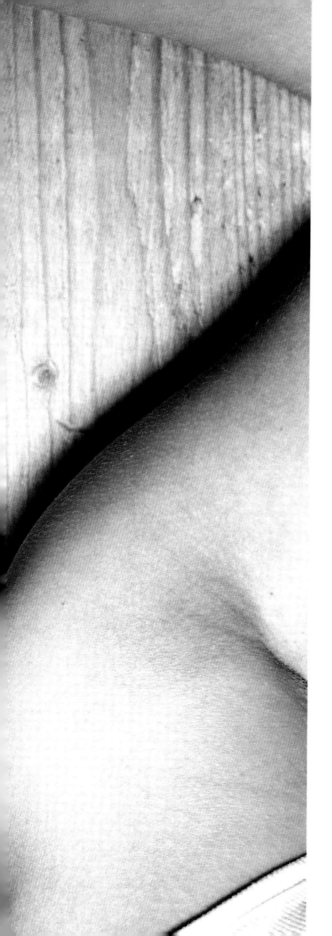

1923

1928

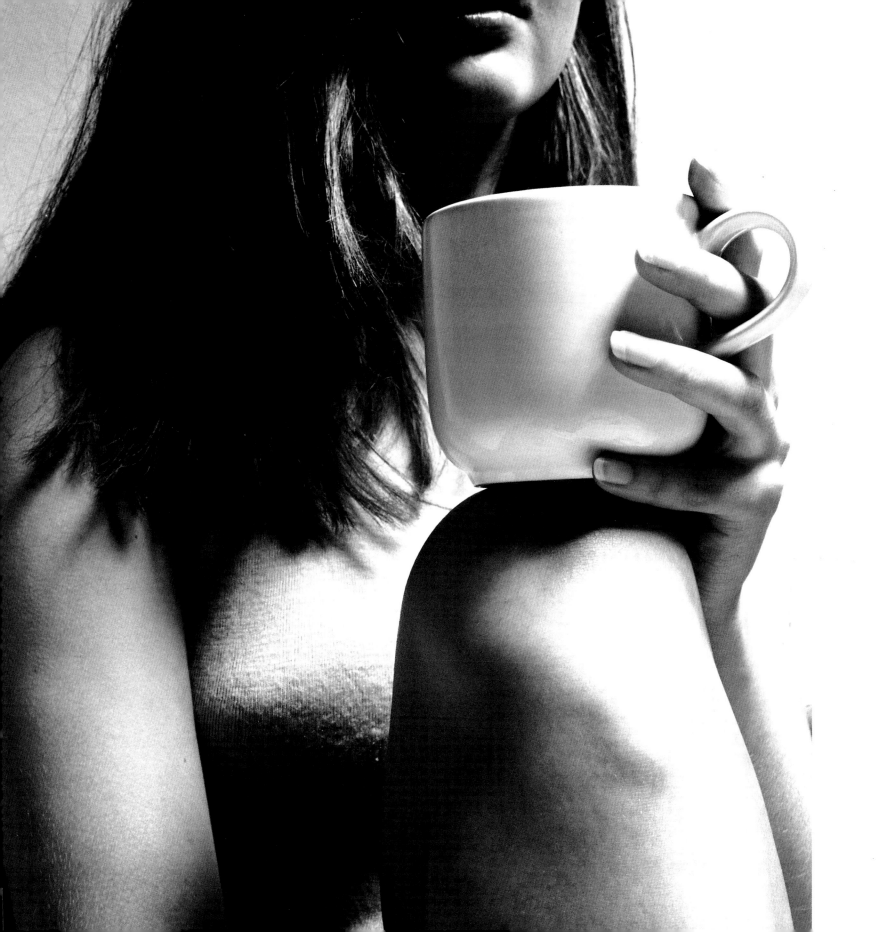

2029

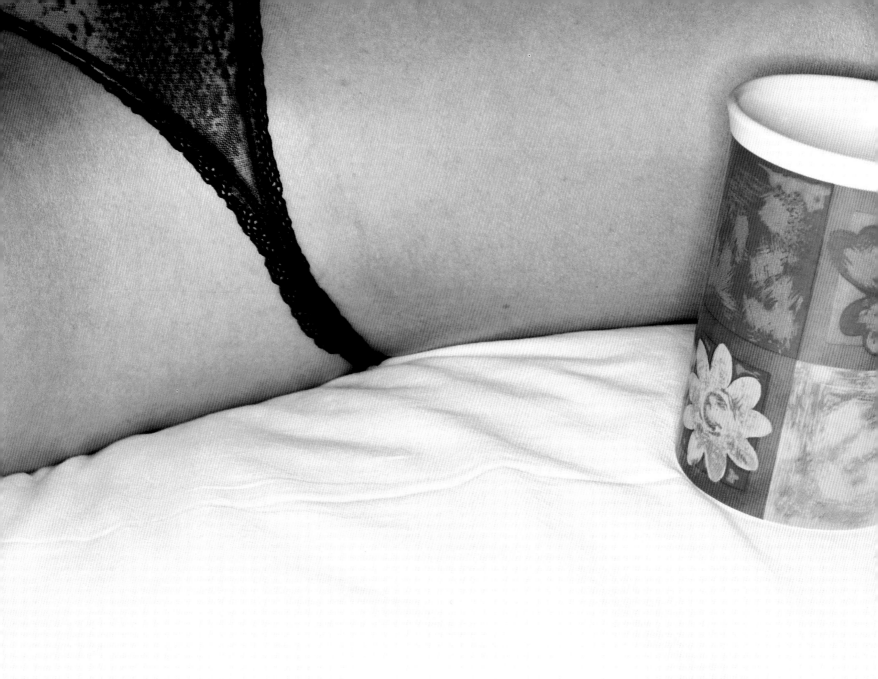

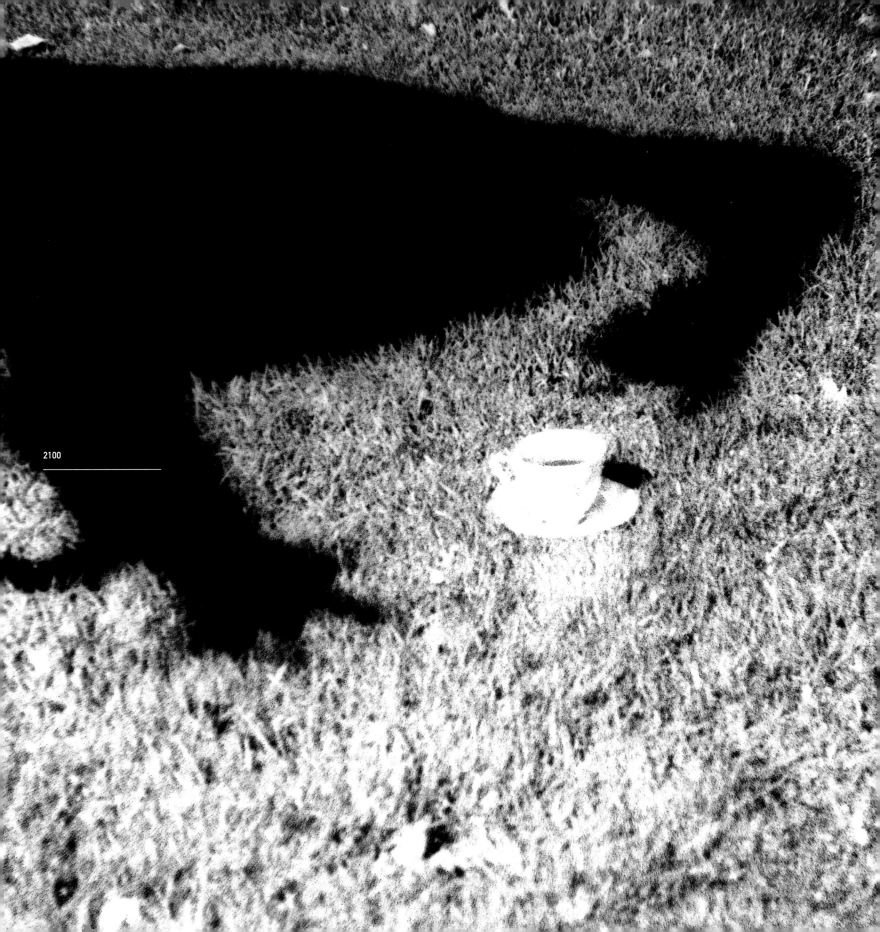

2100

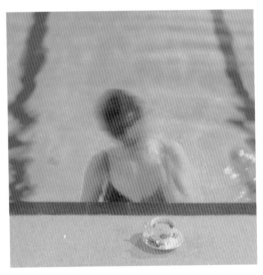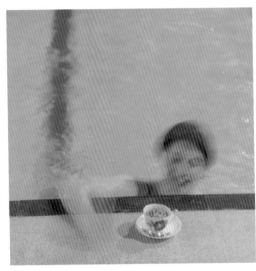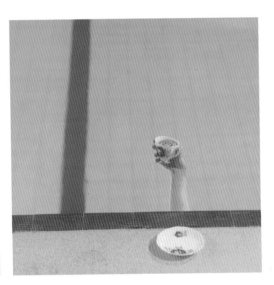

2101-02

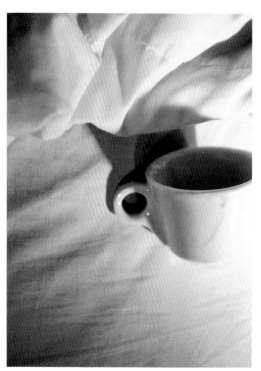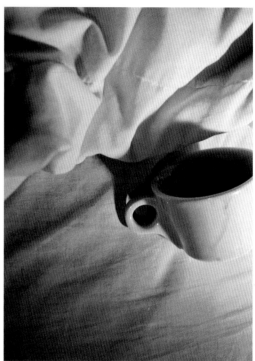

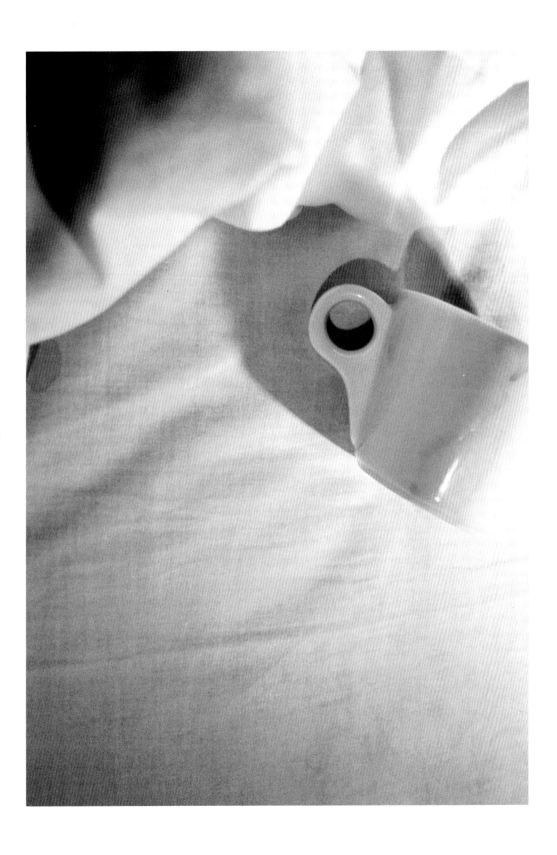

2212/13/16

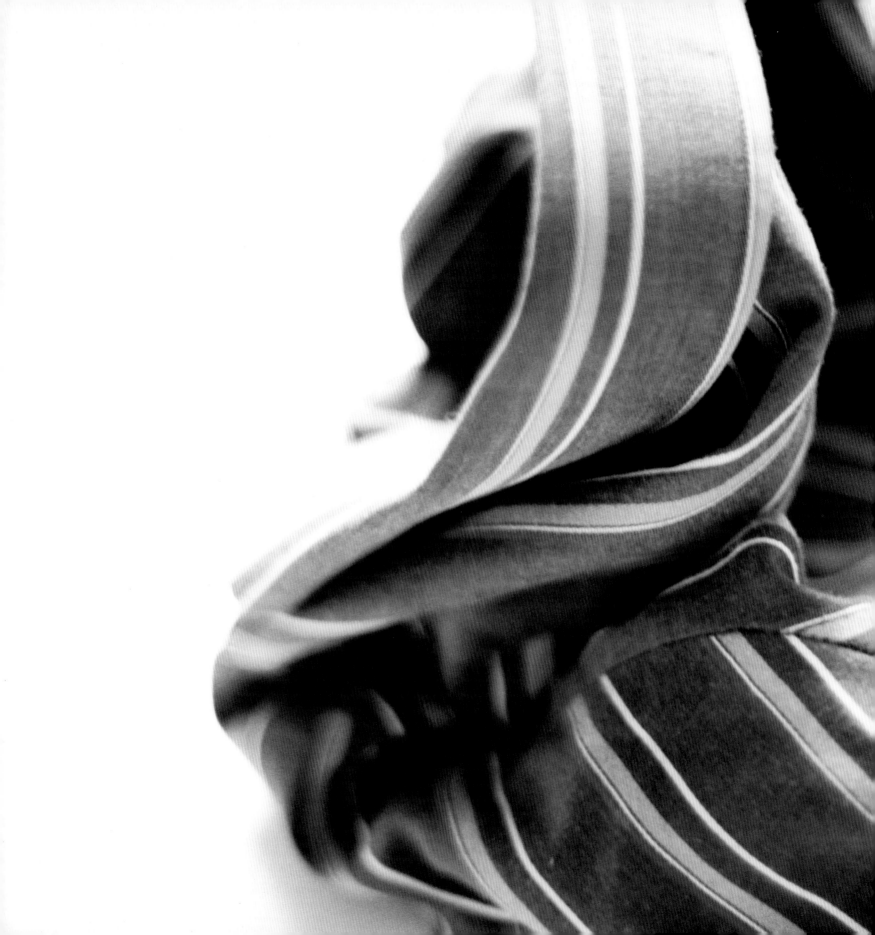

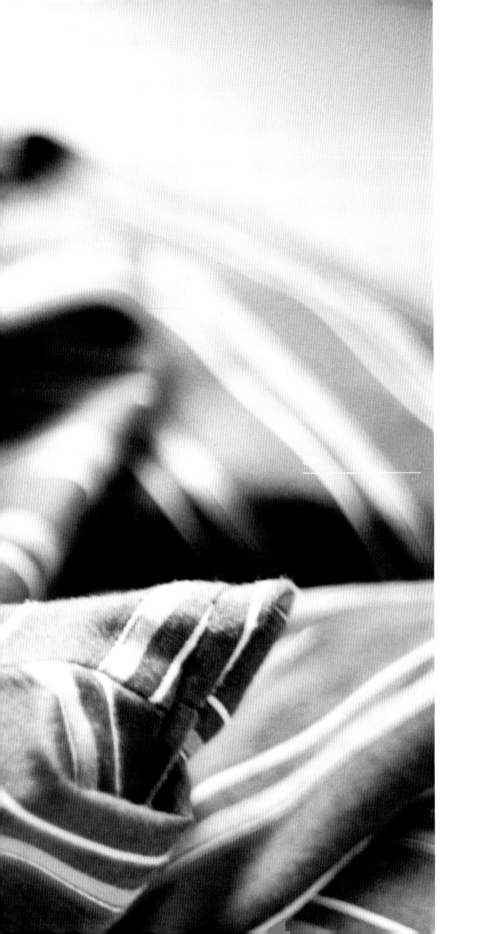

2345

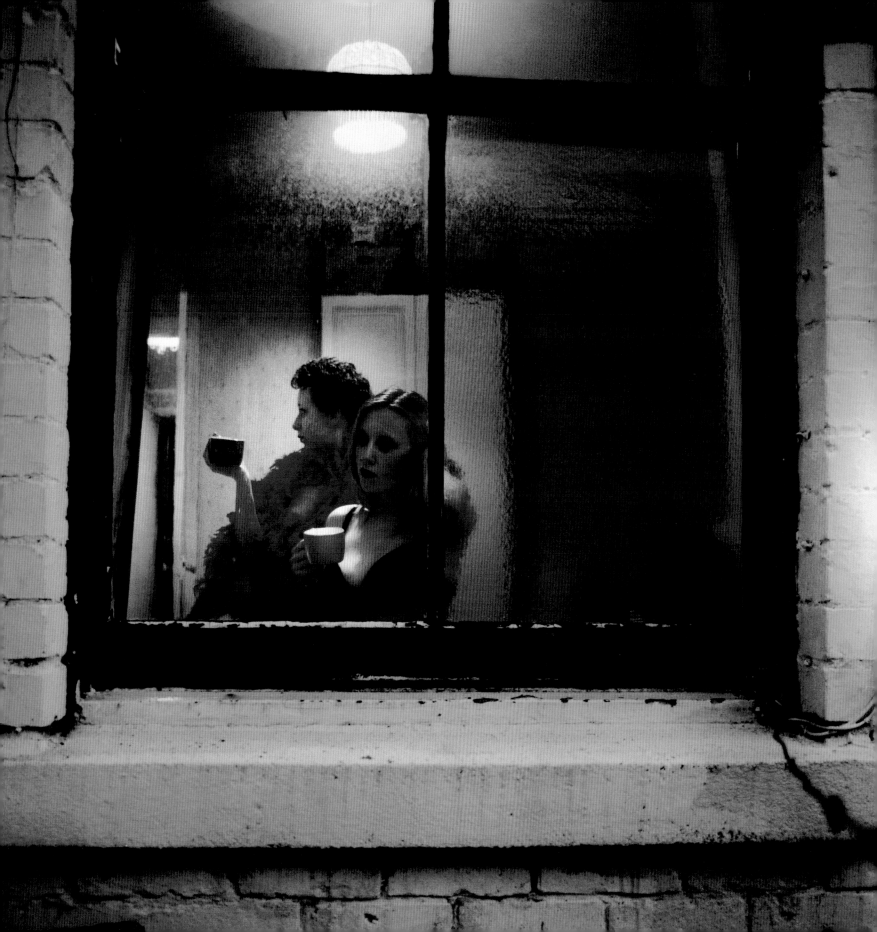

2359

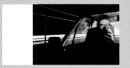 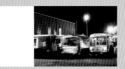 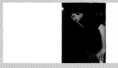 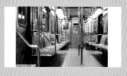 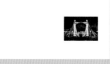 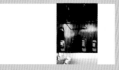

0030
Jenny Moore

0215
Rachael Kearney

0245
Robert Bader

0246
Jane F Stockdale

0414
Jamie Harris

0426
Jane F Stockdale

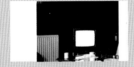 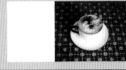 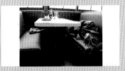 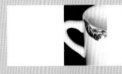 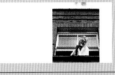 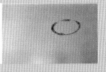

0500
Graham Carrick

0735
Annie Collinge

0800
Anna Rosa Krau

0944
Rankin

0954
Matt Holyoak

1004
Jamie Harris

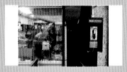
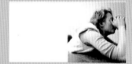
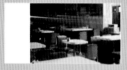
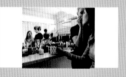
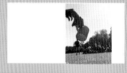
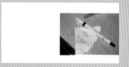

1006
Jane F Stockdale

1030
Anna Rosa Krau

1032
Simon Barber

1137
Jamie Harris

1155
Matt Holyoak

1203
Niki Kennedy

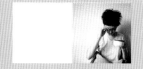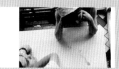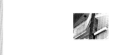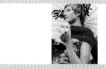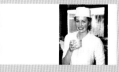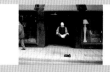

1315
Peter Guenzel

1400
Kenny McCracken

1412
Jamie Harris

1430
Thomas Johnson

1439
Henry Andrews

1504
Tomas Valenzuela

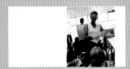 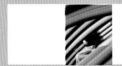 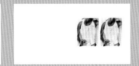 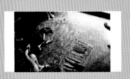 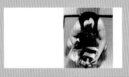 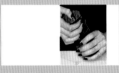

1509
Jamie Harris

1532
Katya & Alexie Sommer

1537 45/46
Rankin

1600
Linnea Larsson

1617
Matt Holyoak

1618
Rankin

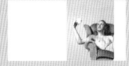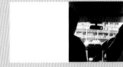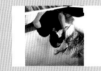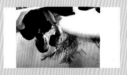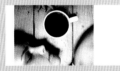

1648
Jamie Harris

1740
Rankin

1831
Laurie Bartley

1834
Laurie Bartley

1923
Daron Bailey

1928
Daron Bailey

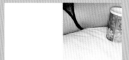 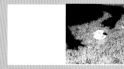  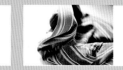 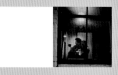

2029
Rankin

2100
Tapani Huovinen
& Cordula Glenk

2101/02/03
Tapani Huovinen
& Cordula Glenk

2312/13/16
Laurie Bartley

2329
Jamie Harris

2345
Jonathon Walton

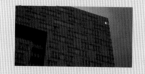

Cover
Stephen Beasley

tick tock tick tock tick tock tick tock tick tock tick tock tick tock tick tock tick tock tick tock tick tock tick tock tick tock ticktock tick tock tick tock tick tock tick tock tick tock tick tock tick tock tick tock tick tock ticktock tick tock tick tock tick tock tick tock tick toc tick tock tick tock tick tock tick slurp ticktock tick tock tick tock tick tock tick tock tick tock tick tock tick tock tick tock tick tock ticktock tick tock tick tock tick tock tick tock tick tock tick tock tick tock tick tock tick to

Design	Nuisance
Reprographics	AJD Colour Ltd
Print	Godfrey Lang
Production Manager	Steve Savigear
Production Editor	Emily Moore
Managing Editor	Dan Ross

tick tock tick tock tick tock tick tock tick tock tick tock tick tock tick tock tick tock tick tock ticktock tick tock tick tock tick tock tick tock tick tock tick tock tick tock tick tock tick tock tick tock tick tock tick tock ticktock tick tock tick tock tick tock tick tock tick tock tick tock tick tock tick tock tick tock tick slurp ticktock tick tock tick tock tick tock tick tock tick tock tick tock tick tock tick tock tick tock ticktock tick tock tick tock tick tock tick tock tick tock tick tock tick toc

24 hours first published in Great Britain in 2000 by Vision On Publishing Ltd in association with Dazed & Confused Magazine 112-116 Old Street London EC1V 9BG T +44 207 336 0766 F +44 207 336 0966 visionon@visiononpublishing.com

Photography by Henry Andrews, Robert Bader, Daron Bailey, Simon Barber, Laurie Bartley, Stephen Beasley, Graham Carrick, Annie Collinge, Cordula Glenk, Peter Guenzel, Jamie Harris, Matt Holyoak, Tapani Huovinen, Thomas Johnson, Rachael Kearney, Niki Kennedy, Anna Rosa Krau, Linnea Larsson, Kenny McCracken, Jenny Moore, Rankin, Alexie Sommer, Katya Sommer, Jane F Stockdale and Jonathon Walton

Photographic copyright © 2000

The right of Henry Andrews, Robert Bader, Daron Bailey, Simon Barber, Laurie Bartley, Stephen Beasley, Graham Carrick, Annie Collinge, Cordula Glenk, Peter Guenzel, Jamie Harris, Matt Holyoak, Tapani Huovinen, Thomas Johnson, Rachael Kearney, Niki Kennedy, Anna Rosa Krau, Linnea Larsson, Kenny McCracken, Jenny Moore, Rankin, Alexie Sommer, Katya Sommer, Jane F Stockdale and Jonathon Walton to be identified as the authors of their work has been asserted by them in accordance with the Copyright, Designs and Patents Act of 1988.

ISBN 19033990 X 0

Special thanks to Giles Hirst, Catherine Stuart, Tanya Lake, Grace Opong, Andy Duffin, Colin Passmore, Guy Isherwood, Wai Hung Young, Colin Cooper and Kirk Teasdale for their invaluable assistance on this project.

tick tock tick tock tick tock tick tock tick siurp ticktock tick tock tick tock tick tock tick tock tick tock tick tock tick tock tick tock tick tock tick tock tick tock ticktock tick tock tick tock tick tock tick tock tick tock tick tock tick tock tick tock tick tock tick tock tick tock tick tock tick tock tick tock tick tock tick tock tick tock tick tock ticktock tick tock tick tock tick tock tick tock tick tock tick tock tick tock tick tock tick tock tick tock tick tock ticktock tick tock tick tock tick tock tick tock

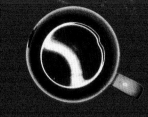

tick tock tick tock tick tock tick tock tick slurp ticktock tick tock tick tock tick tock tick tock tick tock tick tock tick tock tick tock tick tock tick tock ticktock tick tock tick tock tick tock tick tock tick tock tick tock tick tock tick tock tick tock